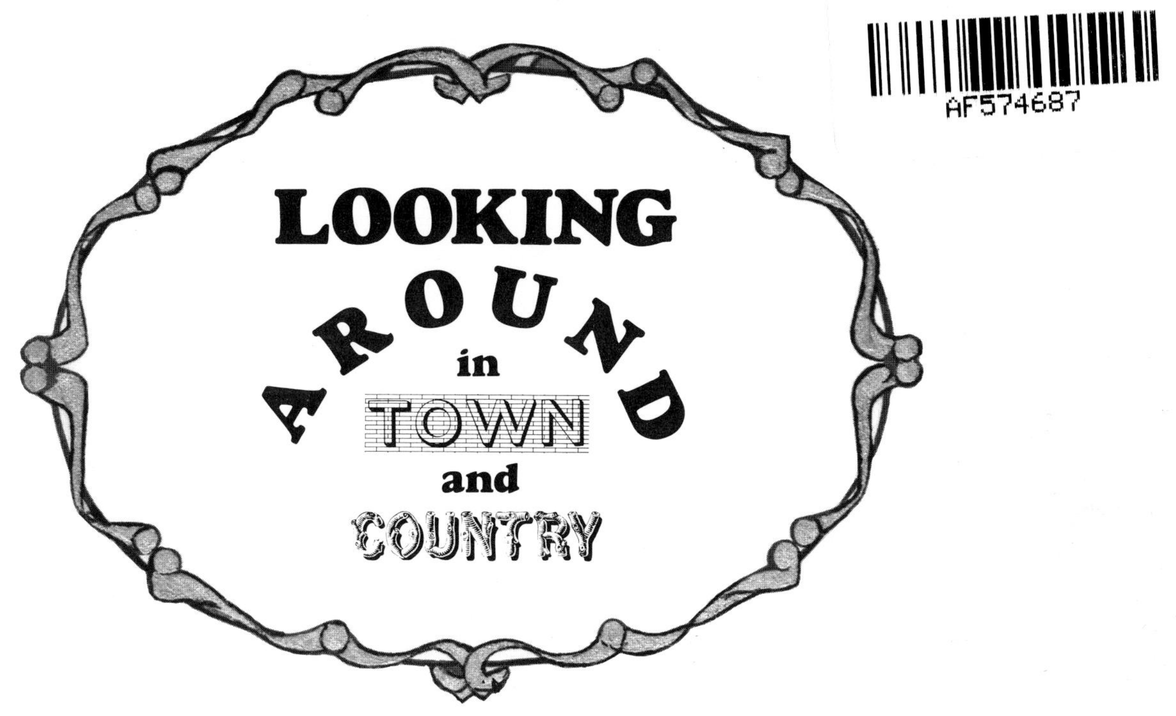

PHILIP SAUVAIN

FRANKLIN WATTS
London

CONTENTS

How to use this book

This pictorial guide to the environment aims to help you identify and find out more about many of the fascinating things you may see about you on a day's outing, a journey, a holiday, or even simply on the way home. As well as a general reference and source book, it can be used to answer three main types of questions:

1. I THINK THAT'S A PACKHORSE BRIDGE, ISN'T IT? *If you know (or think you know) what the object is and want to confirm your guess and find out more about it,* the ALPHABETICAL INDEX with more than 1000 entries (pages 155-161) will enable you to find quickly the page on which the item is mentioned, usually accompanied by a picture. So if you see what you think is a rood screen in a church, pages 64-65 will confirm it, and page 75 will show that that farm implement is a hay turner also called a "cock pheasant". Equally, if you want to find out what a Percheron horse looks like (whether you can see one at the moment or just want to extend your knowledge), the alphabetical index will quickly give you the reference you need.

2. THAT'S A BRIDGE, BUT WHAT KIND? *If the object you are trying to identify is part of or like something of which you do know the name,* the ALPHABETICAL INDEX can help again, especially since major references are printed in capitals, or you can use the CONTENTS. Many things can be identified by looking up the appropriate subject reference, for example, "*Bridges*" (pages 114-5), "*Doorways*" (page 23) or "*Canals*" (pages 128-9). So if you see an ugly sculptured head on the outside of what you know to be a church, look up "*Church Features*" (pages 64-5) and you can identify it as a gargoyle. If you see a cow and want to know what kind it is, "*Cattle Breeds*" on page 80 should help you. To help further, the Contents is divided into four sections ("TOWN"; "COUNTRYSIDE"; "HILLS, VALLEYS, ROUTEWAYS"; "COAST") according to the type of country where the topics covered are normally found, so if you want to find out more about some feature of a river, look up "*Rivers*" under the "HILLS, VALLEYS, ROUTEWAYS" section, and pages 110 and 111 should help you. As a further help,

headings under each section or sub-section are printed in the same kind of type. Of course, it cannot always be obvious which is the right section, since churches, for example, can be found in towns, in the countryside, at the coast and on hills, so sometimes you will have to hunt a little, or turn to the Alphabetical Index.

3. WHAT'S THAT OVER THERE? *You have no idea what the object is, nor what it is associated with (or you are too far away to see!)* Then try the PICTURE INDEX at the back of the book. This has over 130 miniature pictures of items often confused with each other. The pictures have been arranged in sections according to their outward shape and appearance, i.e. posts; crosses; obelisks and stone pillars; metal towers and masts; shelters; walls; round towers; rectangular and square towers; other buildings; rocks and stones; mounds; slopes; valleys; bowls and hollows; water features; signs and marks; other features. So if you see in the distance, for example, a tall metal round tower looking rather like a fat cigar, you can turn to the Picture Index and under the heading "ROUND TOWERS" you will find the miniature picture of a *silo*. By referring to page 78 (the section on farm buildings) the picture of a silo on that page will confirm your guess and the text explains that a silo is used for storing silage—green crops (usually grass) shredded into fragments and stored as animal fodder.

Good hunting!

PHILIP SAUVAIN

Thanks are due to the following for permission to reproduce copyright material:

Aerofilms, 7, 43, 85, 87 (top), 95, 135; J. Allan Cash, 17 (top left), 34 (top), 60 (bottom right), 61 (bottom right), 101; Ashmolean Museum, Department of Antiquities, 39 (bottom right); Colin Bord, 67 (top right); Janet Bord, 67 (top left); British Steel Corporation, 32 (bottom left); British Tourist Authority, 92 (top right, bottom left and right), 123 (centre); Central Office of Information, 34 (bottom left); Department of the Environment, 70 (bottom right), 73, 89 (bottom left), 124-5; Margot Davies, 92 (centre); Ford's, 32 (bottom right); Geological Museum, 99 (top and second from top), 103 (bottom left and top centre), 134 (middle and bottom), 143 (top left); London Brick Co. Ltd., 33 (bottom right); Museum of English Rural Life, Reading, 91 (all except top left); National Monuments Record, 88 (bottom); Reed Paper and Board Co. Ltd., 33 (top row, centre); Shell Photographic Service, 32 (top); Dean and Chapter, Westminster Abbey, 64 (top right).

Other pictures are author's or publisher's copyright.

TOWN

PANORAMA OF A TOWN

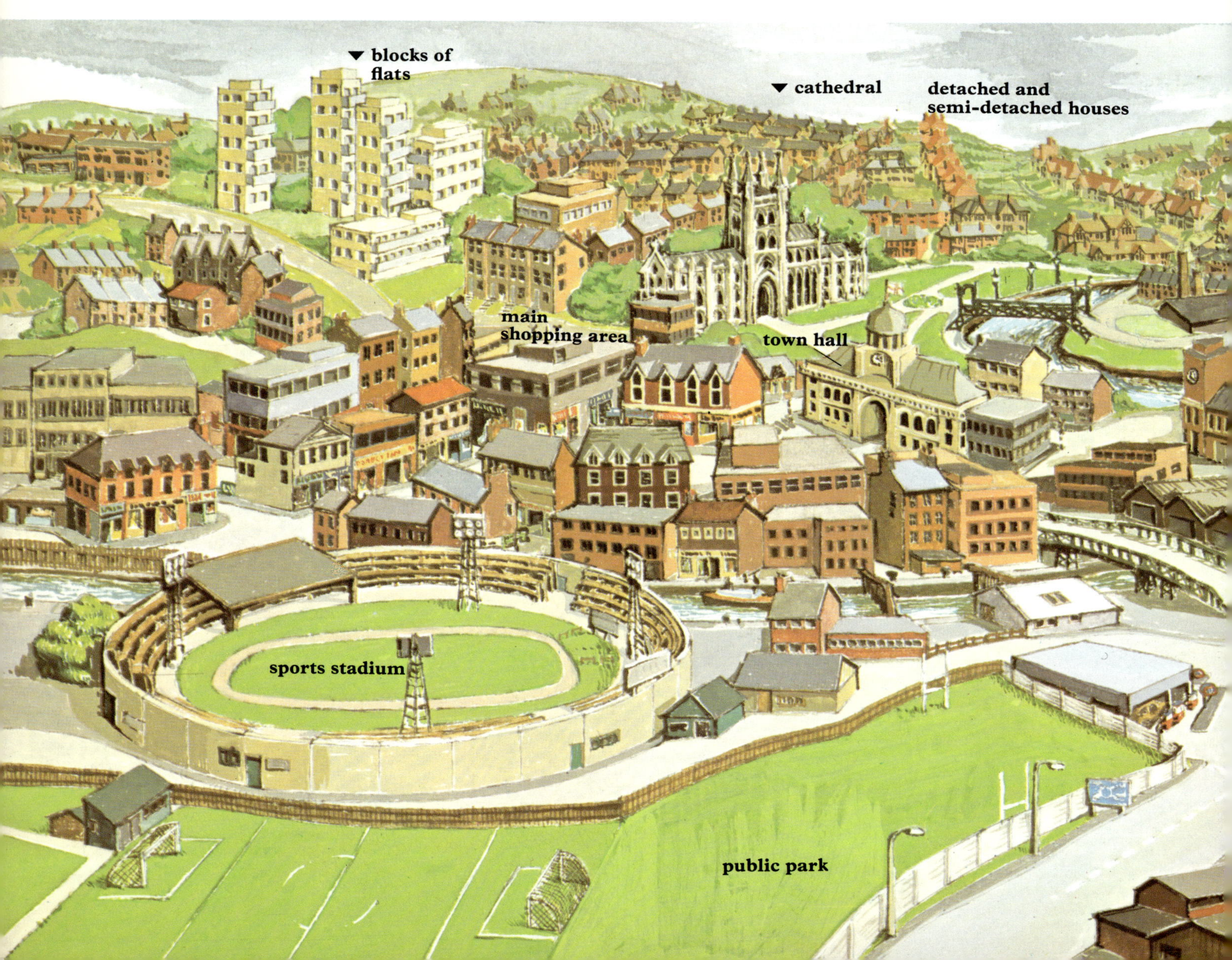

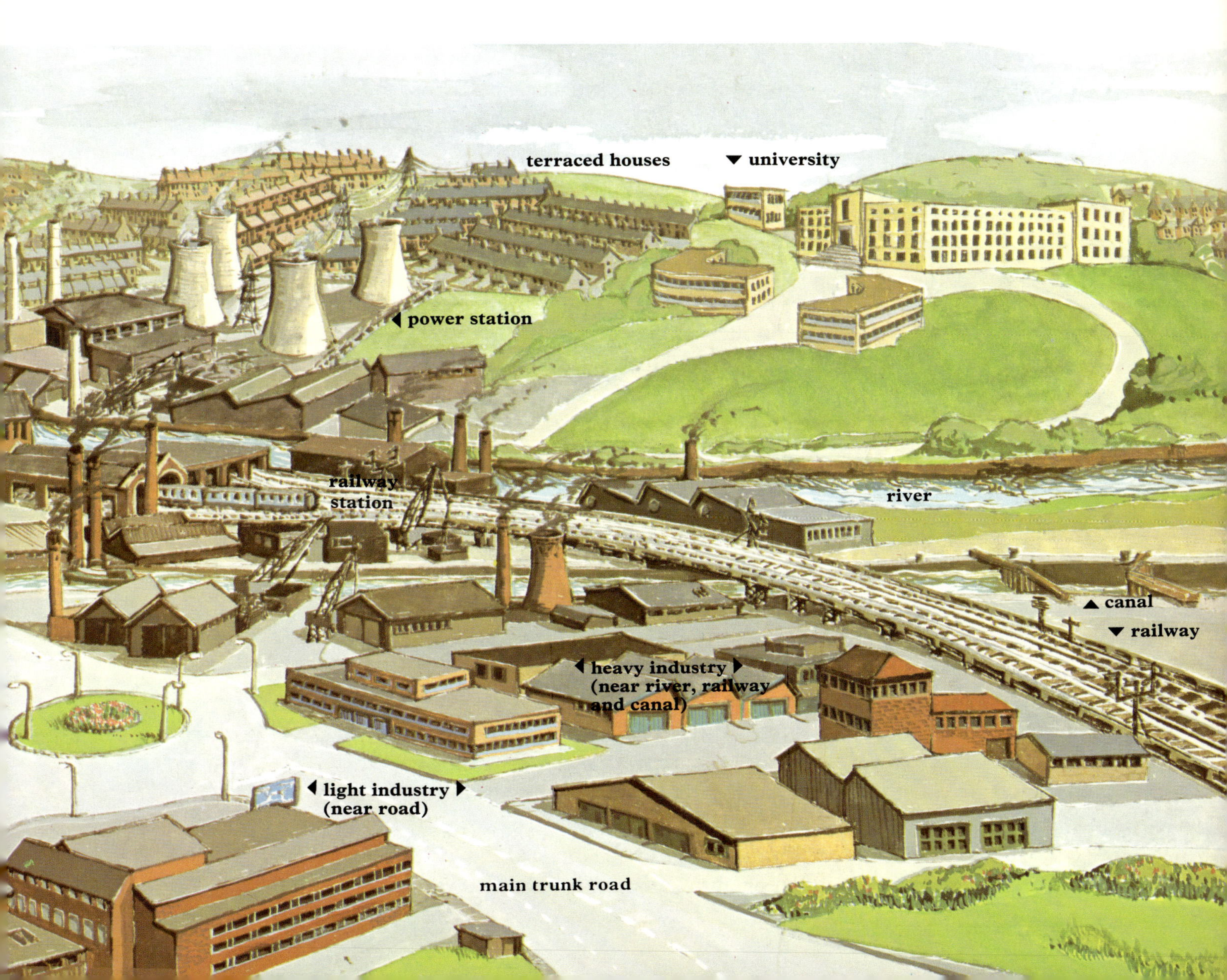
terraced houses
university
power station
railway station
river
canal
railway
heavy industry (near river, railway and canal)
light industry (near road)
main trunk road

A TOWNSCAPE

▲ Richmond, Yorkshire

The centre of a town can often be divided into different areas or zones. In one area you can find most of the banks, insurance offices and building societies; in another part you can find all the big stores; in other areas you can find most of the local government offices, or the cinemas and places of entertainment. The town centre is often the oldest part of the town, although nowadays redevelopment schemes often make the centre look as if it is the newest.

From a distance, at dawn or at dusk, the town's buildings may be silhouetted against the sun. The character of a town can often be seen in townscapes like the one below where a cluster of tall buildings show the town centre, and high-rise flats and church towers punctuate the surrounding areas of houses, shops and industrial premises. ▼

TYPES OF TOWNS

Most towns do a number of jobs, such as providing a shopping centre for the surrounding area, or housing the offices of large companies and local government departments. Other functions include industry, communications, entertainments and educational services (for example, schools and colleges). Some towns are largely residential with many people going to work in nearby centres, some towns are specialists such as a port, a railway junction, a seaside resort, a mining town, an administrative centre or a town dominated by a cathedral or a university. Most towns, however, have several functions to perform and when a town is described as being of a particular type (say, a market town) this is done purely in order to identify its most important or distinctive characteristic.

▲ industrial town

▲ market town

▲ tourist centre

▲ port

▲ cathedral city

▲ residential area

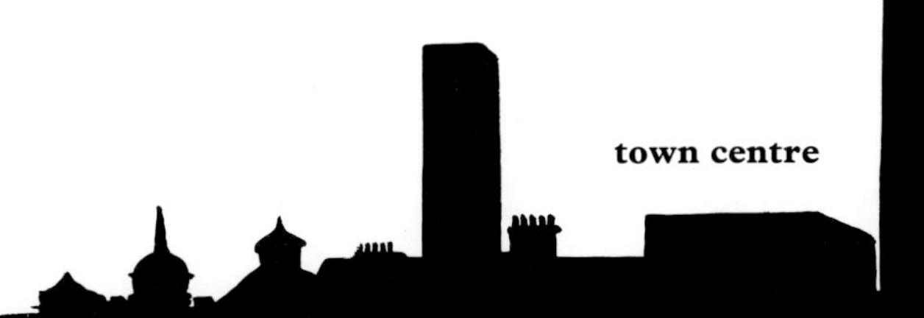

town centre

SIGNS OF THE PAST

Wherever you look in a town you will see signs of the past — a mason's marks on a wall perhaps, or a plaque, statue, effigy, datestone, memorial or even a trade sign of the past.

Masons' marks and property marks such as crosses, letters and symbols are sometimes seen on old houses and churches.

mason's marks

Datestones must always be treated with a certain amount of caution. Sometimes the stone has been removed from another building or the stone indicates the date of an extension to the main building.

▲ datestone

▲ barber's pole

Trade signs are rare sights these days. In the past they advertised the type of shop in the same way that an inn sign indicates a public house. A red and white striped pole indicated a barber's shop and three brass balls advertised the pawnbroker's.

Effigies, monuments, statues and memorial brasses often tell us a lot about the costume, weapons and customs of the past. Effigies and brasses are usually found in churches.

▲ war memorial

TOWN DEFENCES

The remains of medieval town walls can sometimes be seen today. At King's Lynn, the southern approaches to the town were guarded by the South Gates. In many towns the gateway is the only reminder of the days when the town had walls. Extensive remains can be seen, however, in some towns, especially York. Many towns had castles and to this day carry names which remind us of this (Newcastle-upon-Tyne, Castleton and Castleford). Some towns were built on defensive sites such as the summit of a hill or inside the meander of a river (for example, Durham and Shrewsbury).

◀ rubbing from a brass

▲ town gateway

▼ town wall

OLD BUILDINGS

Most towns, however new or industrial, have old buildings several hundred years old. The function of many of these buildings is not always apparent to the eye.

Guildhall ▶

▲

The Guildhall was the headquarters of a medieval guild of craftsmen. Since those days it may have been adapted for other purposes, such as a school or town hall.

▲ **old grammar school**

▲

Many grammar schools were founded in Tudor times. The old buildings have usually long since been replaced by modern school premises and often incorporated in comprehensive schools, but the old school buildings still stand as a monument to the past.

Almshouses were founded by rich men to provide homes for old people. They are often long low buildings. Many almshouses date back to the seventeenth century.

▼

▼ **almshouses**

▲ Station Hotel

▲ Town Hall

The Victorians erected many solid ugly buildings. In their own way they reflect this period of middle-class prosperity, respectability and newly-won wealth. The Corn Exchange, the Railway Station, the Station Hotel, the Town Hall and the Nonconformist Chapel usually present particularly good examples of Victorian building design.

▼ railway station

STREET NAMES

A town's street names often tell its history. Streets may recall former politicians such as Gladstone, Peel and Asquith. Most towns in Britain have streets named after Queen Victoria and Prince Albert. Street names often bring back past events, for example, battles such as Waterloo and Trafalgar. Former trades are recalled by Weaver Street, Baker Lane, Tanner Row, Mercer Lane. Some names recall entertainments (the Bull Ring) or punishments (Gallowgate). Frequently the streets in the centre of a town have the medieval ending "gate" meaning street (Kirkgate, Stramongate, Westgate). Many streets were named after features such as buildings, woods, sources of water supply and common land (Castle Road, Wood Lane, Well Lane).

London Road
HAYMARKET
JUBILEE AVENUE
WESTGATE
MILL LANE
Kirkgate
Well Lane
Baker Street
SEBASTOPOL TERRACE
Gladstone Road
THE SHAMBLES
PEEL STREET
CRIMEA ROAD
VICTORIA TERRACE
Bull Ring
Castle Road

STREET FURNITURE

This is the name given to the ornaments, posts and miscellaneous features to be found in streets.

fountain ▶

◀ spur stone

A spur stone protected the corner of a building from damage by vehicles.

Fountains were often erected by public benefactors to give a healthy source of drinking water to the street.

Foot scrapers enabled visitors to remove the thick coating of mud they carried on their boots after walking along streets in the days before good pavements and motor roads.

▲ cobblestones

Cobblestones still pave some streets, particularly where there are steep slopes. The cobbles give a better grip in icy weather.

▲ railings

▼ foot scraper

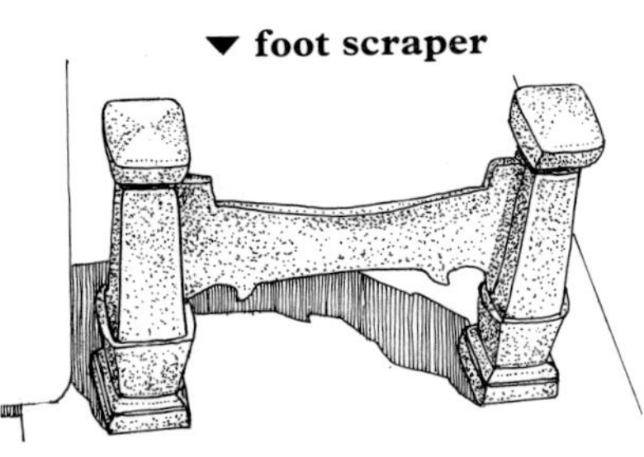

▲ bollard

Traffic bollards protected pedestrians on the pavement.

Railings often add a decorative touch to the street apart from protecting property.

▲ **mews cottages**

Mews cottages are converted from the stable blocks of a hundred years or so ago. Often they are in a backstreet because they backed onto fine town houses which formed the main thoroughfares. Today they are often fine modern homes.

Pillar boxes reveal their age by the royal monograms on them. Most towns have examples of letter boxes with Queen Victoria's monogram.

▼ **pillar box monogram**

▲ **hydrant sign**

The yellow hydrant sign shows an outlet fitted to the mains water supply specially for the use of firemen. The numbers indicate the diameter of the water pipe and the distance to the manhole cover above the outlet pipe.

Lamp posts are a good example of changing tastes and fashions. Sometimes old gas lamps can be located.

▼ **lamp post**

KIRKBY STEPHEN MARKET

NOTICE IS HEREBY GIVEN,

THAT BY VIRTUE AND UNDER THE PROVISIONS OF THE CHARTER GRANTED BY EDWARD III IN THE YEAR OF OUR LORD, ONE THOUSAND THREE HUNDRED AND FIFTY TWO, TO GEORGE, EARL OF CUMBERLAND AND HIS HEIRS, THE FOLLOWING REGULATIONS SHALL BE ENFORCED AND THE FOLLOWING TOLLS AND STALLAGES, SHALL BE TAKEN IN RESPECT OF STALLS, STANDS, SHOWS, AUCTIONS, OR SPACES OCCUPIED BY PERSONS EXPOSING GOODS FOR SALE OR OTHERWISE IN THE MARKETS OR FAIRS OF KIRKBY STEPHEN.

1– For every Person Standing or Walking exposing Commodities of any Kind for Sale on handbarrow or other Vehicle not occupying any defined space, one Penny and upwards.

2– For every Bushel (Customary Measure) of Potatoes exposed for sale in the Market, One Toll-Dishfull.

3 For every Stall or Stand whereon the Owner exposes anything for Sale, a Stallage Toll as follows, Viz – four feet long or under 2d and One-Half Penny Per foot for every additional foot occupied.

4– For each set of Hobby Horses, Swing Boats or Bicycles, Propelled by Steam, Hand or Horse

▲

Noticeboards often throw interesting light on the past.

▼

Manhole covers and drain covers tell us what services are under our feet. They often have interesting designs.

▼ **manhole cover**

HOUSES

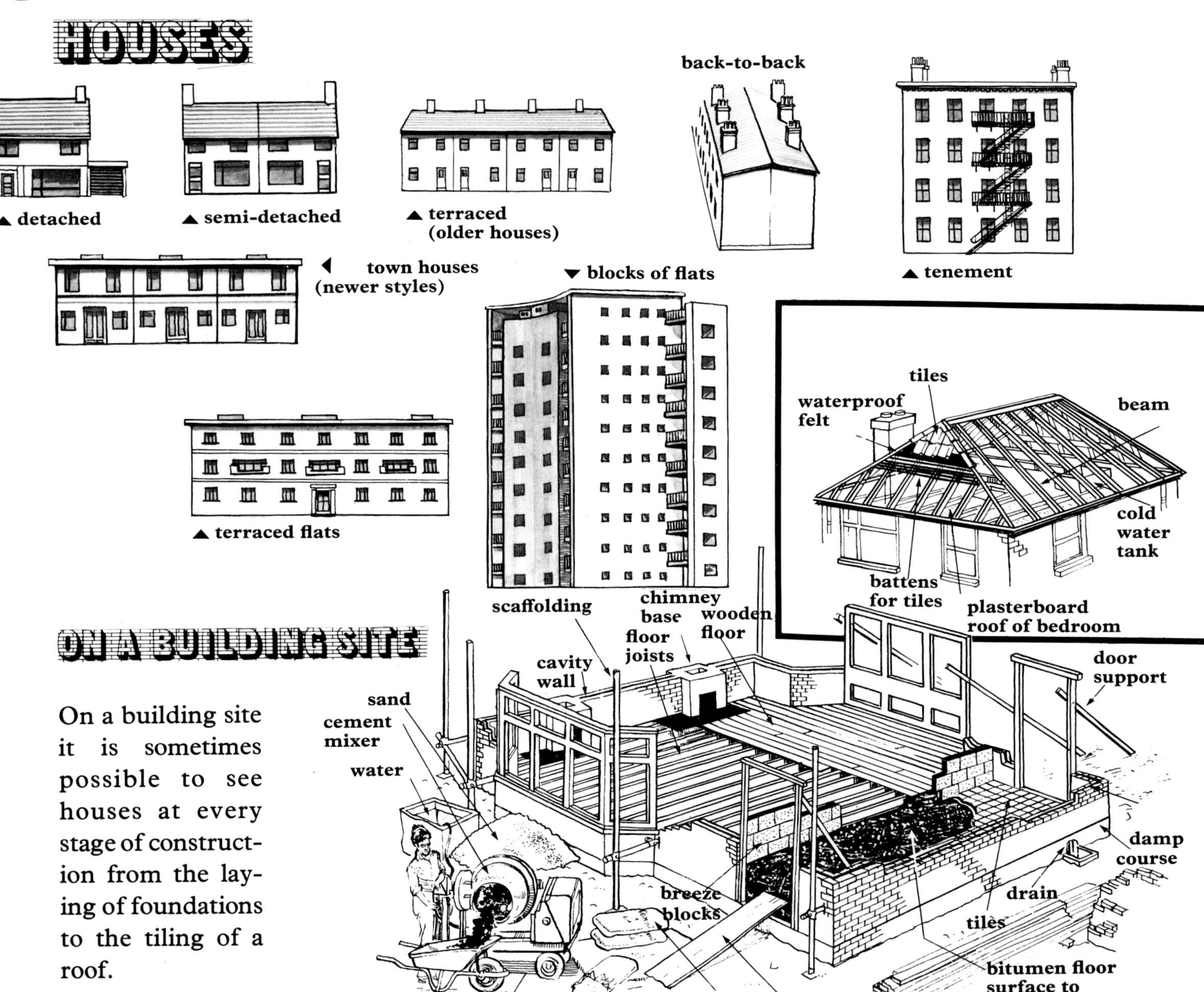

ON A BUILDING SITE

On a building site it is sometimes possible to see houses at every stage of construction from the laying of foundations to the tiling of a roof.

FEATURES OF A HOUSE

In many ways the basic techniques of building a house have hardly changed since Tudor times. Some of the technical terms used to describe the different features of a house are shown on page 18 (for new houses) and on this page (for an eighteenth century mansion).

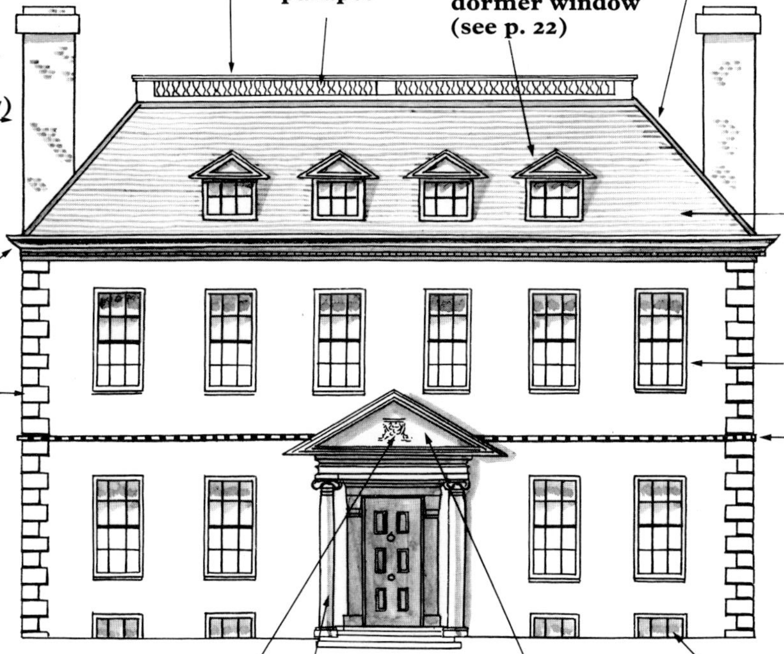

balustrade (railing supported on small pillars or balusters)

parapet

dormer window (see p. 22)

hipped roof (see p. 26)

chimney stack (see p. 27)

attic

eaves

sash window (see p. 22)

quoins (corner stones—one long stone and then one short)

string course (an ornamental line)

escutcheon (shield bearing a coat of arms)

portico (porch supported by pillars or columns)

pediment (a triangular gable above a door or window—the space enclosed is called the tympanum)

basement

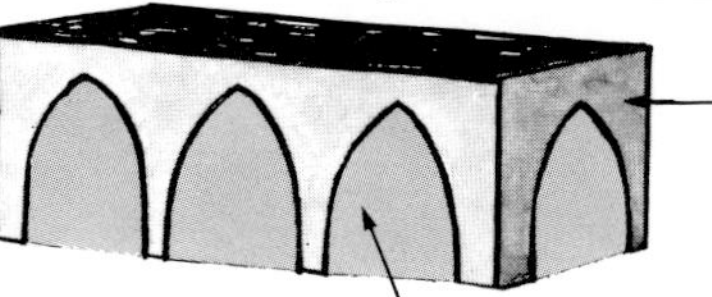

loggia (arcade which is open on one side)

arcade (a series of arches)

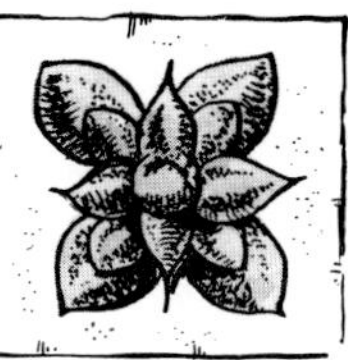

bas relief (a carving on a wall which stands out in 3D)

corbelling—stonework or brickwork built outwards to support a structure such as an oriel window (see p. 22)

cupola (a small dome)

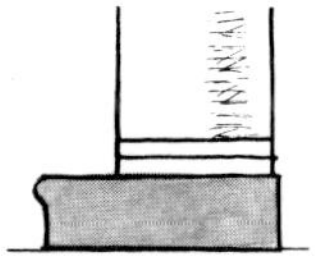

plinth (projecting base of column or building)

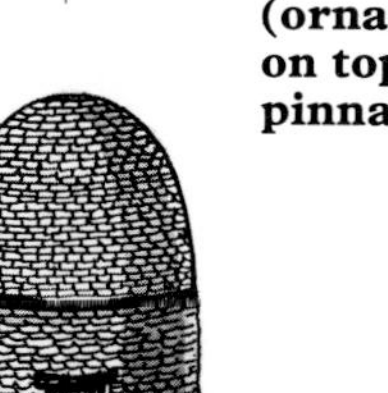

finials (ornament on top of pinnacle)

rotunda (domed circular building)

HOUSE STYLES: Tudor and Elizabethan

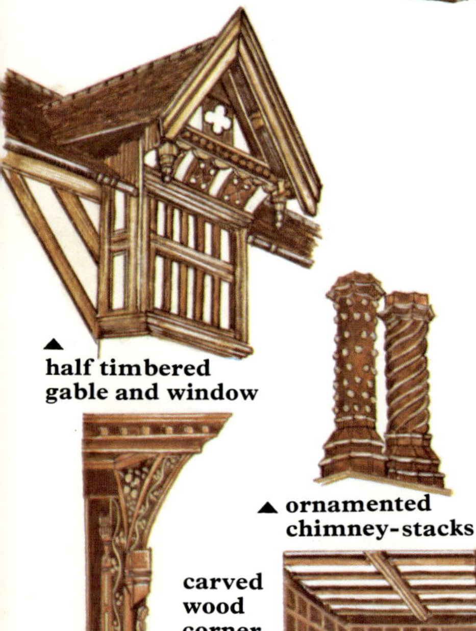

▲ half timbered gable and window

▲ ornamented chimney-stacks

carved wood corner post

The age of a house can often be guessed after a careful look at its style of building. Tudor, Elizabethan and early Jacobean houses of the sixteenth and early seventeenth centuries have distinctive and easily recognisable brickwork and timber-work. The use of timber frames (see page 57) with their studs and jetties is characteristic—but beware twentieth-century imitation Tudor houses.

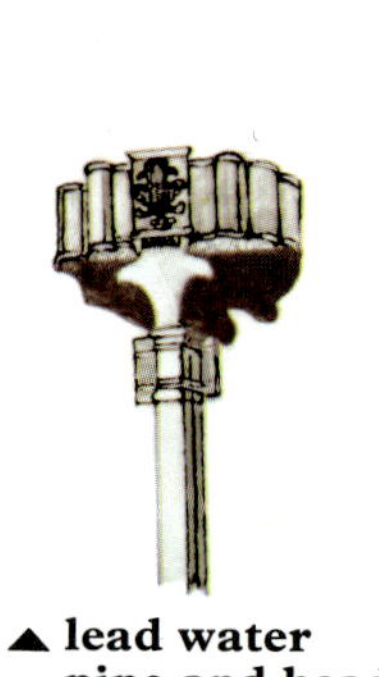

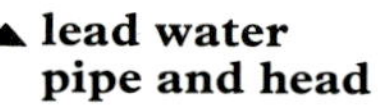

▲ lead water pipe and head

▲ staircase

parapet with heraldic finial ▶

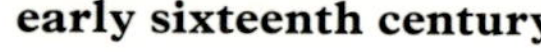

early sixteenth century

◀ oak-panelled rooms ▶

late sixteenth century

HOUSE STYLES: Stuart and Queen Anne

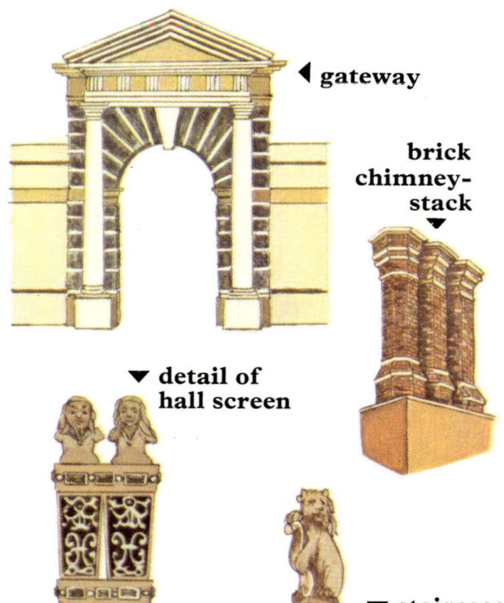

◀ gateway

brick chimney-stack ▼

▼ detail of hall screen

In the past, as today, builders followed the latest fashion when designing houses. Sash windows were introduced towards the end of the seventeenth century, and they became a desirable feature in the houses built after that period. However, it often took many years for new ideas to reach the provinces and for this reason superseded fashions often persisted in remote areas. So similar styles in different parts of the country are not necessarily exactly contemporary.

▼ doorway

▼ sash window

carved decoration ▼

▼ staircase

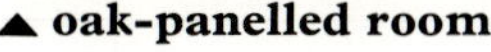

▲ oak-panelled room

WINDOWS

gable

▲ gabled dormer (in slope of roof – see p. 19)

mullion

lintel ▶

◀ transom

sill ▶

pane

light

mullions

▲ mullioned window

hinged at one end

arched centre window

round or oval window

▲ leaded lights

▲ casement

▲ Venetian

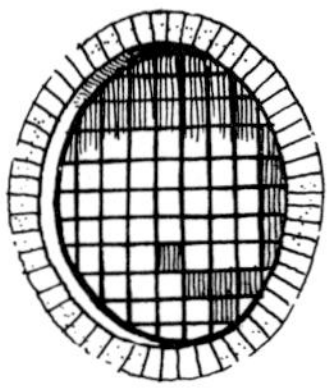

▲ oculus

window slides up and down

curved

▲ sash

▲ oriel

corbelling

▲ bow

square or slanting sides

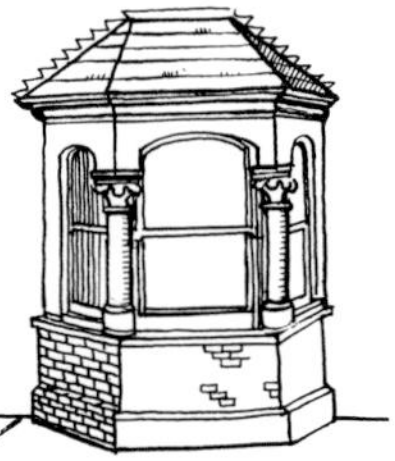

▲ bay

The earliest windows did not have glass panes, but in the sixteenth century glass became relatively common, at least in the larger mansions. **Panes** are often small, either square or diamond in shape, and set within lead frames. These are called **leaded lights.** The **light** is the opening formed by the window supports and can consist of a number of separate panes of glass. When they divide the window opening into a number of lights, the vertical supports are called **mullions**. The horizontal supports which are needed for tall windows are called **transoms**.

Sixteenth century and early seventeenth century windows are often long, horizontal, mullioned windows. A window hinged at either end to open outwards or inwards is called a **casement** window. **Bay** windows were popular in Tudor times. The **oriel** window (a bay window for an upper floor only) was particularly characteristic. In the late seventeenth century **sash** windows were introduced. These are generally tall and suited the tall rooms of the Queen Anne and Georgian periods. Bay windows were not characteristic of the seventeenth and eighteenth centuries, but became typical features of Regency houses in the early nineteenth century—particularly in the form of the **bow** window.

DOORWAYS

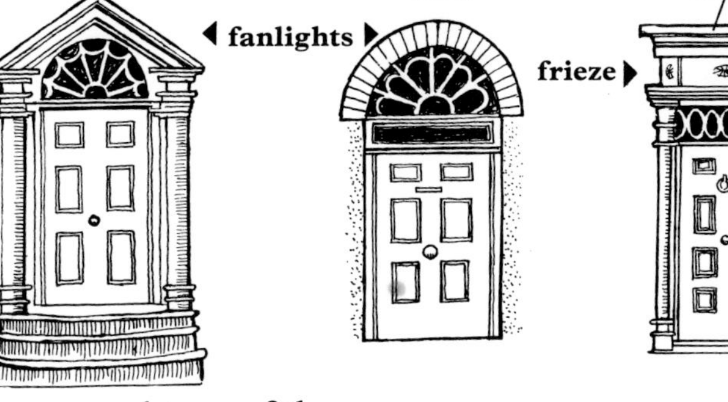

Doors vary according to the age and type of the house. The door of a medieval cottage is very plain when compared with the ornate and splendid entrance to a Georgian mansion. The older the house the plainer the doorway. In the medieval period some doors were mounted on hinges or brackets fitted directly on to the timber or stone walls of the house. Door frames became increasingly common in succeeding centuries and the sides of the doorway (the **jambs**) were sometimes carved. They often project beyond the wall of the house in an elaborate moulding. The vertical stone or timber strut across the top of the door frame (the **lintel**) was sometimes decorated. It is often marked with a date, initials or other markings. In the eighteenth century it is often part of an **arch** or **pediment** or **canopy**. There are often **fanlights** set above the door to throw light into the hallway. There are other features to be identified such as **keystones, pilasters, porticos** and **shell-canopied** doorways.

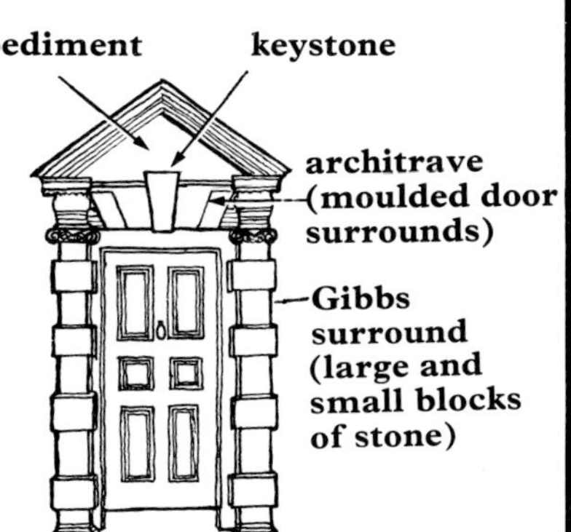

STAIRCASES

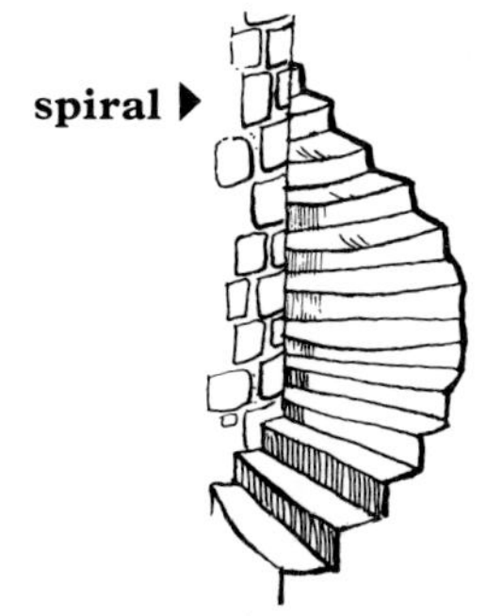

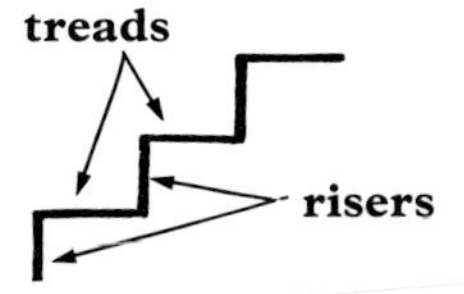

HOUSE STYLES: GEORGIAN AND PALLADIAN

plaster panel ▶

◀ cupola

Houses of the Queen Anne period and the eighteenth century are often distinguished by **hipped roofs** (see also page 26) and by the use of large blocks of stone on the corners of the walls called **quoins** (see also page 56). The term **Palladian** is often used to describe houses of the eighteenth century which copied a style derived from a sixteenth-century Italian architect called Palladio.

▲ doorway

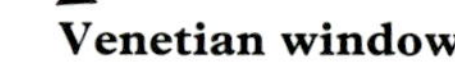

▲ Venetian window

▼ urn

▲ entrance gateway

▲ room with plaster mouldings

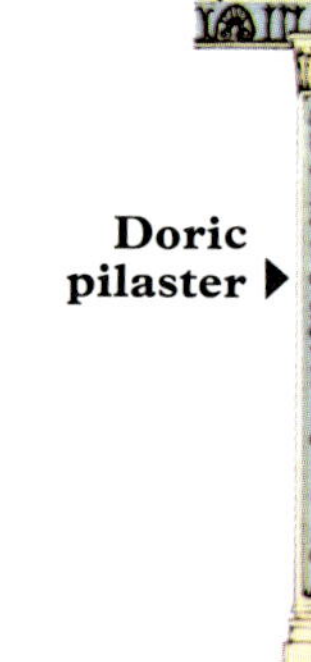

Doric pilaster ▶

HOUSE STYLES: Regency

▲ fireplace

▲ ornament

▲ interior door

▲ exterior door

▲ iron pier

The Regency period takes its name from the Prince Regent (1811-1830). The distinctive characteristics of this architectural style are elegant **terraced houses, crescents, wrought iron railings, balconies** and **bow windows.**

▲ elegant interior (a picture gallery)

ROOFS

The simplest form of roof is flat, but in a wet climate this is not very efficient in getting rid of rain water. A **single pitch** roof can be used, but for most houses some form of **double pitch** roof has been chosen. The ends of such a roof are called **gables.**

▲ double-gabled

▲ half-hipped

The roof almost invariably overlaps the walls of the house and where it does is the **eaves.** Sometimes **barge boards** cover the edges of the gable ends. Different types of gable end include the **Dutch gable** introduced in the eighteenth century. In earlier centuries **crow-stepped** gables were common, particularly in Scotland. **Hipped** gables are very common and in some parts of the country **mansard** roofs, **double-gabled** roofs and **half-hipped** roofs are characteristic features. The mansard roof was particularly useful since it allowed greater headroom in the attic space under the roof.

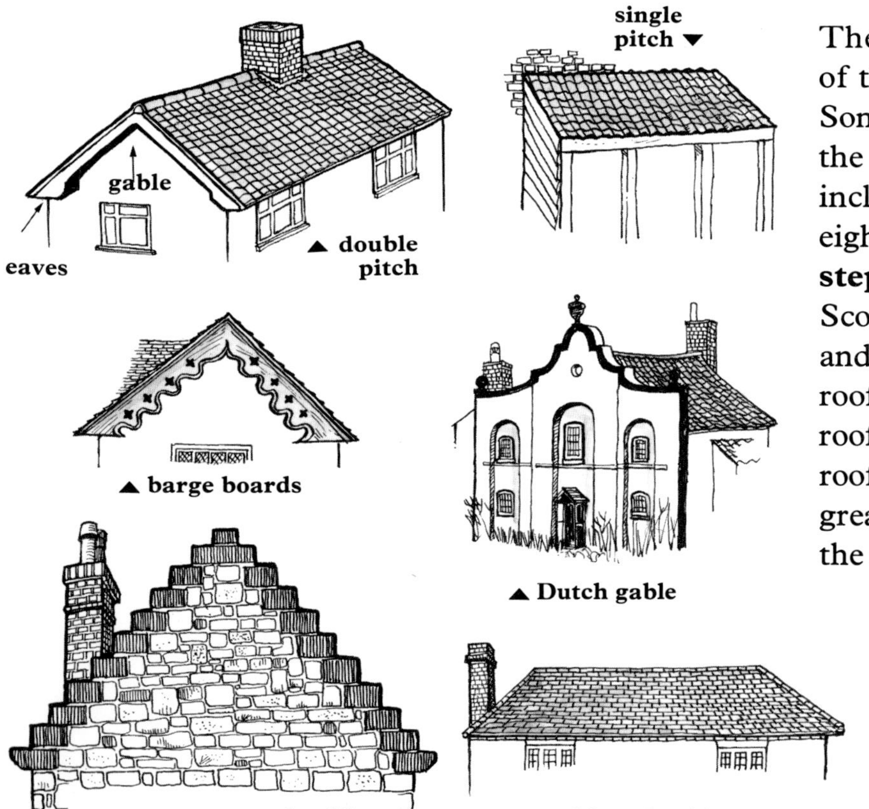

▲ double pitch

single pitch ▼

▲ barge boards

▲ Dutch gable

▲ crow-stepped gable

▲ hipped gable

▲ mansard roof

CEILINGS

The various beams used to construct a timber ceiling and support a roof have special names as you can see from the diagrams. Many of these features are well illustrated in old churches and barns.

KING POST ROOF ▶

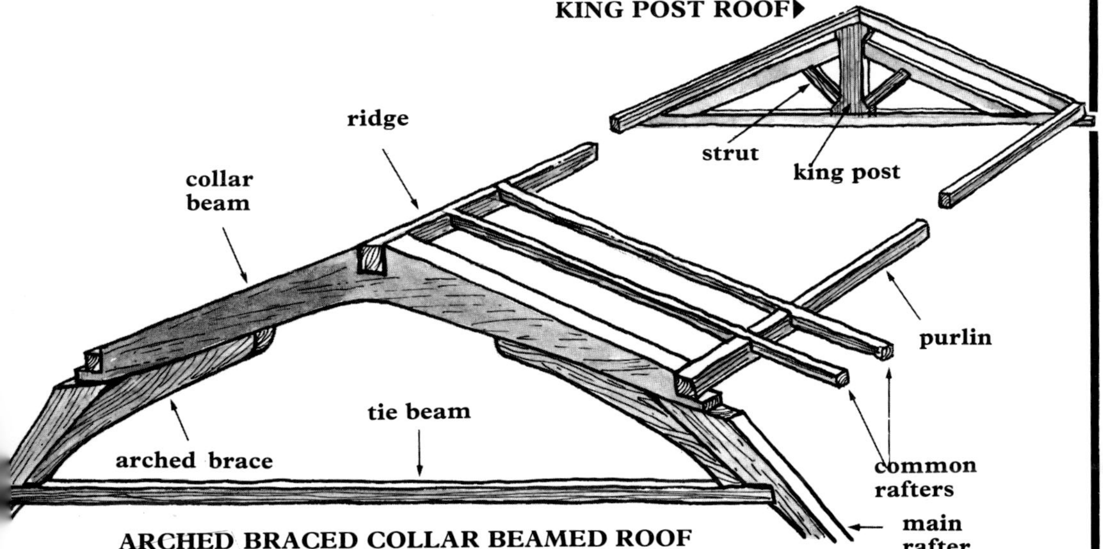

ridge
strut
king post
collar beam
purlin
tie beam
arched brace
common rafters
main rafter

ARCHED BRACED COLLAR BEAMED ROOF

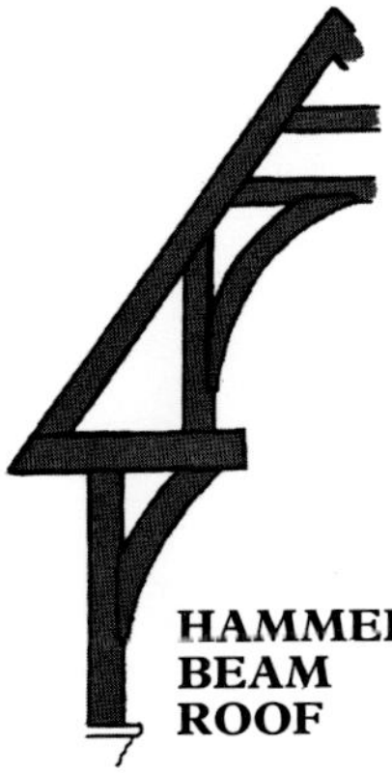

HAMMER-BEAM ROOF

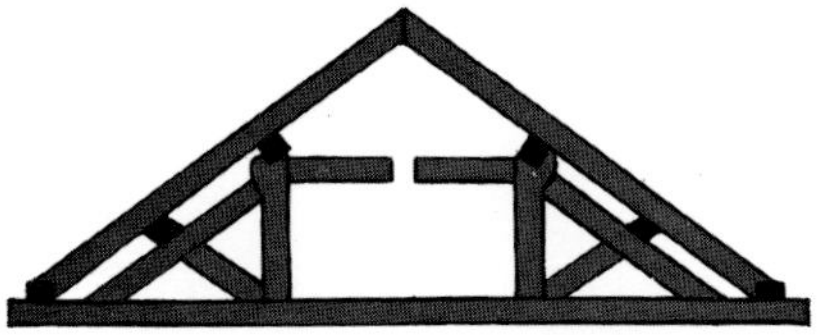

▲ QUEEN POST ROOF

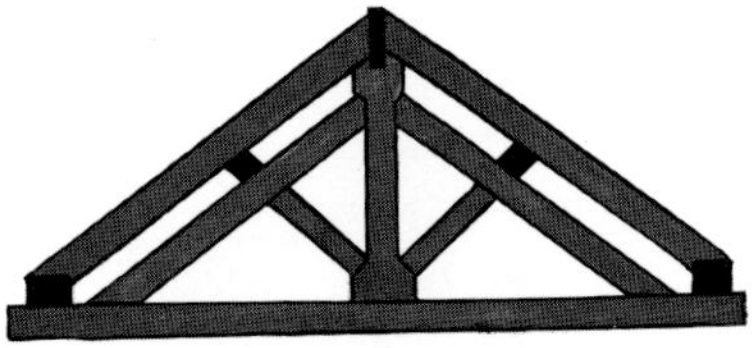

▲ KING POST ROOF

CHIMNEYS

◀ Tudor chimney stacks
stacks
◀ pots

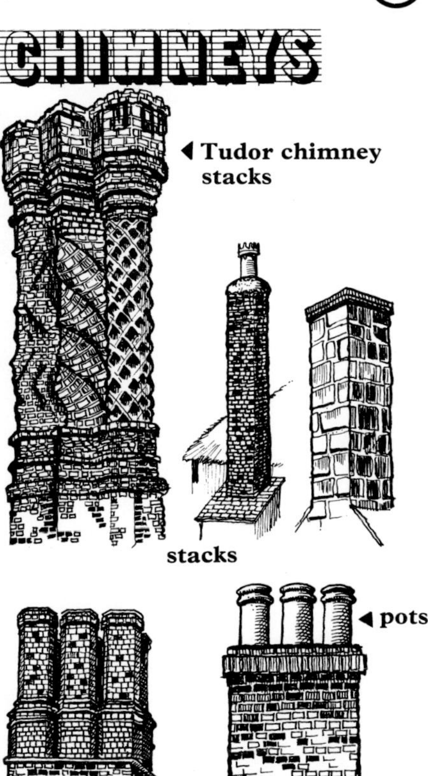

It is often surprising to see just how many different shapes and sizes of chimney stack and chimney pot can be observed within a relatively short distance. The position of the chimney stack varies as does its height and the building materials used. Chimney pots are generally no older than the nineteenth century.

▼ terraces in a Yorkshire mill town

▼ street in Manchester

▼ Gothic windows

▼ bay windows

HOUSE STYLES: Victorian

The Victorian period saw the development of housing for the masses. Although cheap and originally often unsavoury these terraced houses were often sufficiently well built to last well into the twentieth century. Moreover, the rapid rise in population in the nineteenth century meant that much more housing was built in Victorian times than in earlier periods. The dominant house type for the Victorian worker was the terraced house—particularly the back-to-back house. Houses for the well-to-do were often over-elaborate and ornate with features copied from churches of the Gothic period.

HOUSE STYLES: The Twentieth Century

The twentieth century has seen an improvement in housing for the ordinary person. The **Edwardian terraces** with their bay windows were a development of late Victorian styles. After the First World War houses became somewhat plainer in appearance although still featuring the bay window. **Mock Tudor** houses became fashionable for the well-to-do; some experiments were made with **concrete** and **flat-topped** roofs; **semi-detached** houses became common. After the Second World War there was a move to greater simplicity of design and houses were built with plain, unadorned fronts and often large **picture windows.** New building techniques such as industrialised housing, blocks of **flats**, a return to Georgian designs for high cost houses, **open plan** gardens and rows of **town houses** (a development of the terraced house) are all features of the present day period.

▼ 1900's terraced

▼ 1930's semis

▼ 1960's-70's detached

▼ 1960's-70's flats

INDUSTRIES A COLLIERY

Many industrial operations are carried out in or close to the countryside. The three works shown here are as likely to be found in open country as in a town and yet they are basic to the life of towns and without them industry would grind to a halt. Usually the workers employed there travel from nearby towns and in the case of collieries small towns have developed within a rural area to work the pits.

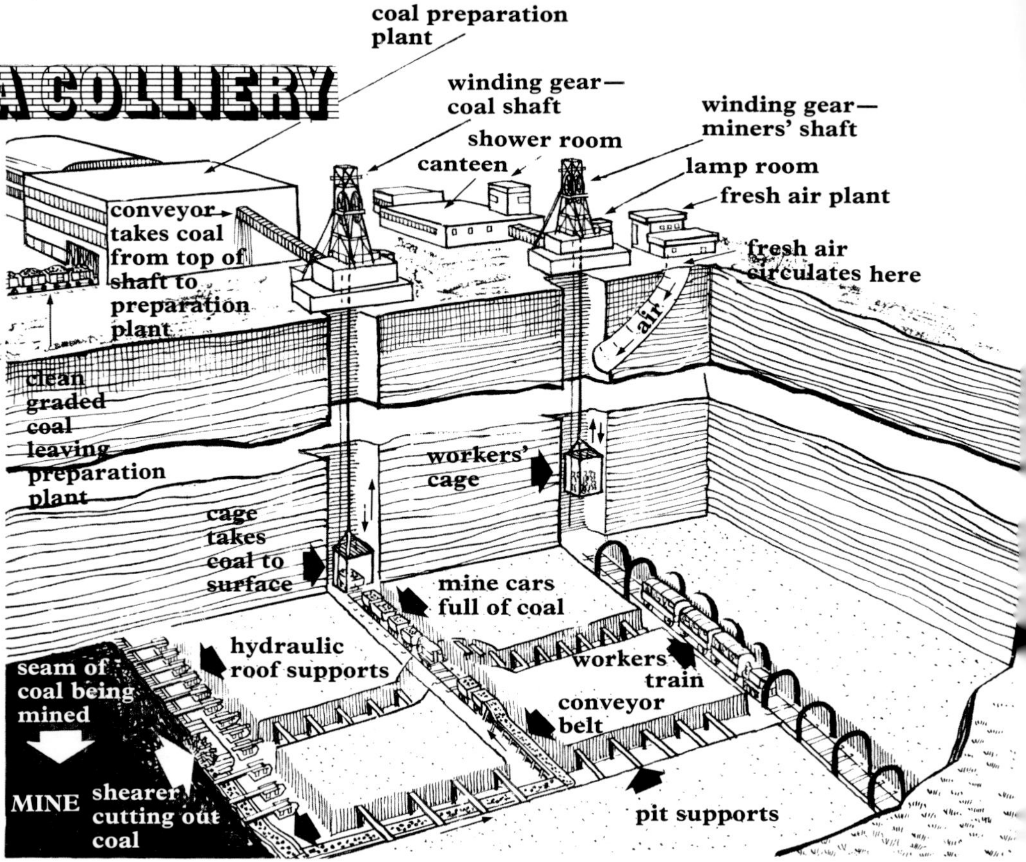

coal preparation plant
winding gear—coal shaft
shower room
canteen
winding gear—miners' shaft
lamp room
fresh air plant
fresh air circulates here
air
conveyor takes coal from top of shaft to preparation plant
clean graded coal leaving preparation plant
workers' cage
cage takes coal to surface
mine cars full of coal
hydraulic roof supports
workers train
conveyor belt
seam of coal being mined
shearer cutting out coal
pit supports

BASIC WORKINGS OF A COAL MINE ABOVE AND BELOW GROUND

The coal industry is changing rapidly. Many pits have been closed and in some cases the only signs of the former coal industry are the cottages and terraced houses built for the miners. More frequently, giant **slag heaps** are a gaunt reminder of the past. But new collieries are being built and these are sometimes difficult to identify as such, because only the telltale **pithead gear** distinguishes them at first glance from other modern factories. If you look carefully, however, it is usually possible to distinguish other features as well such as the **conveyor belt** and the **coal preparation plant.**

◄ coal mine and slag heap

A POWER STATION

This diagram shows a coal-burning power station. You can usually see piles of coal forming miniature pyramids in the **fuel yard.** If they are absent, it is possible that the power station is oil-fired. If you look carefully at the power station you may be able to picture the sequence of processes involved in the production of electricity. The **fuel conveyor belts** take the coal into the **boiler house** and there the boilers heat water to provide steam for the **turbines** which revolve at high speed to produce electric current. Three things are produced: electricity which is taken by the cables supported from **pylons**; **steam** which escapes to be cooled and condensed back into water in the **cooling towers** (and then re-used to produce more steam); and **smoke** released high into the atmosphere from the tall power station **chimneys.**

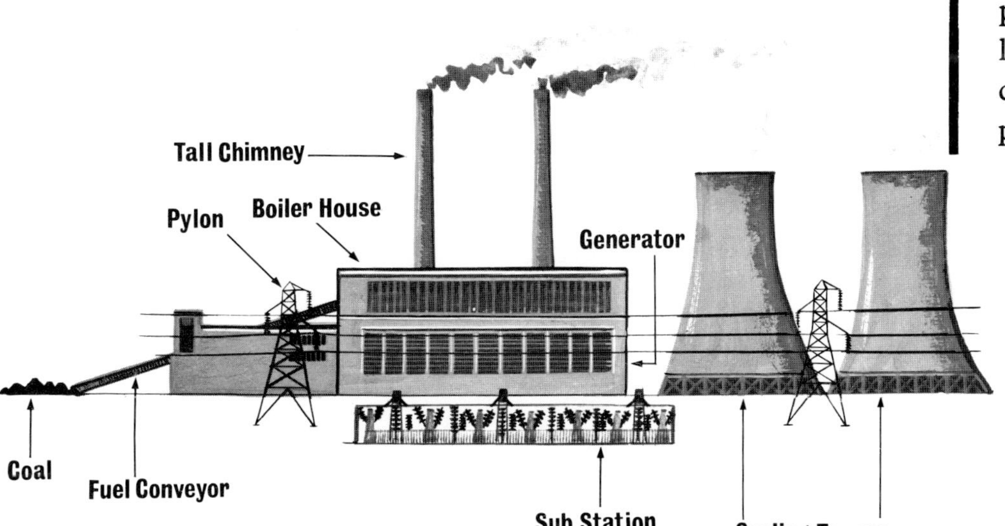

ATOMIC POWER

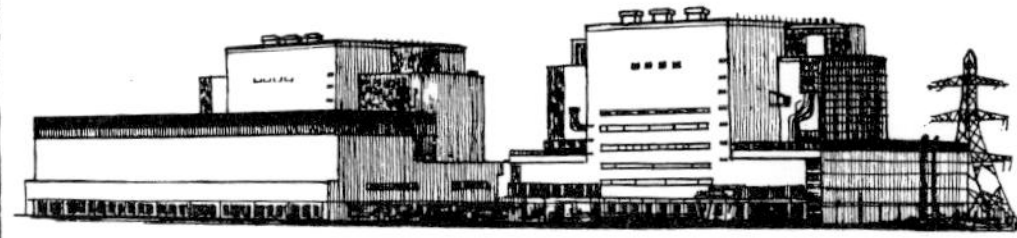

Atomic power stations produce electricity: a **nuclear reactor** provides the heat to make steam to power the turbines. Atomic power stations are usually located at the coast, some distance away from many people.

FACTORY BUILDINGS

The older the factory or works, the easier it is to recognise the type of industry from the appearance of the buildings. On a modern **trading estate** the factories often look so much alike that it is difficult to tell them apart and only the names of the firms, the types of vehicles used (and their cargoes), and sometimes smells and sounds give away the type of product manufactured there. Some industries, however, still have buildings of a distinctive shape and size and some of these are shown in the pictures on these pages.

▼ **oil refinery**

▼ **chemical works**

▼ **steel works: blast furnaces**

▼ **steel works: rolling mill**

▼ **car assembly plant**

▼ **textile mill**

▼ **paper mill**

▼ **salt works**

▼ **shipbuilding**

▼ **sugar refinery**

▼ **slate mill**

▼ **kaolin workings**

▼ **cement works**

▼ **brick works**

INDUSTRIES OF THE PAST

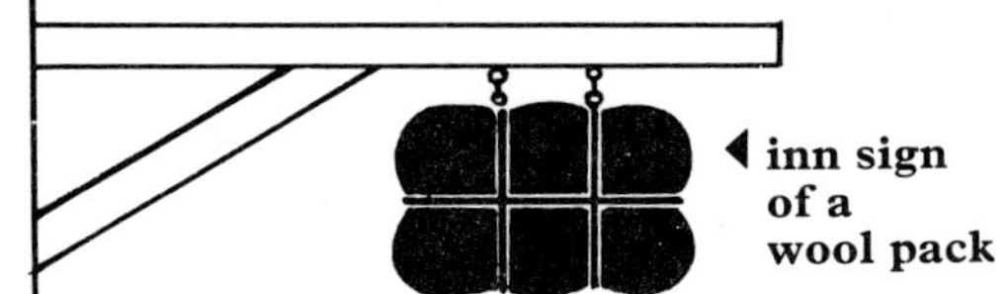

◀ inn sign of a wool pack

▲ Wool Hall, Lavenham

Towns and villages often contain clues to the industries of the past. Sometimes you can see evidence of the woollen industries of the medieval and Elizabethan period such as the Wool Hall shown here, or an inn sign recalling days when the raw material was carried by packhorse. In some areas **weavers' cottages** can be seen with their typical long windows on an upper floor to throw the maximum light possible on the weavers' work in the attic workrooms. In many northern industrial towns old **textile mills** of the nineteenth century can still be seen. These are gaunt, blackened, multi-storey, square buildings with tall chimneys. Sometimes remnants of the old metal-working industries can be seen at the sites of old **forges, bloomeries, hammer ponds** or **iron works.**

▼ weavers' cottages

▼ nineteenth century mill

▼ tin mine

▲ Chimney and mounds of mining debris at Conlig Lead Mines, Northern Ireland

In Cornwall there is still evidence of the tin mines which brought the industrial revolution to the South West over 100 years or so ago.

▲

In Wales, the Lake District and Scotland slate quarries sometimes scar the mountain slopes. Many of these quarries are still in use. Disused quarries gradually fade into the landscape as vegetation covers the workings. Old mine shafts and workings from the past present a hazard to the unwary whether they represent tin, lead, slate, coal, iron, or any other mineral.

▼

slate quarry ▼

In the Peak District of Derbyshire and other Carboniferous Limestone areas the remains of former **lead mines** and **lime kilns** can often be seen on the slopes of the hills.

▼

beehive kilns ▼

▲

At Stoke-on-Trent evidence of the pottery industry of the industrial revolution is fast receding as the picturesque **beehive kilns** which used to fire the pots are replaced by modern **electric** kilns.

OLD MILLS: WINDMILLS

▲ tower windmill

▲ post mill

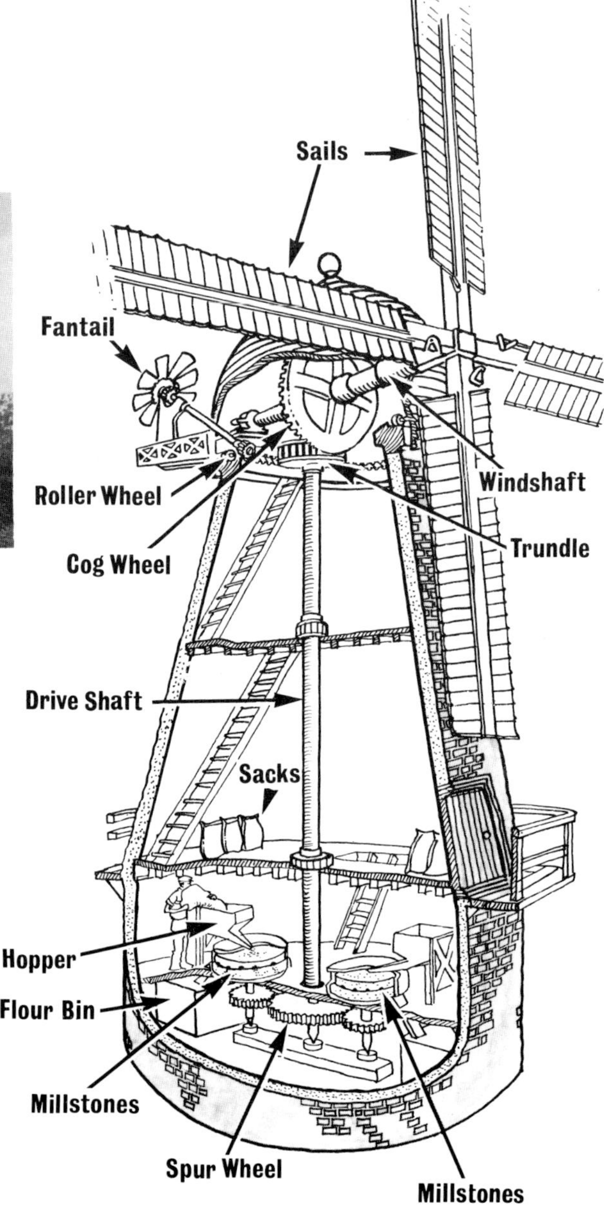

There are two main types of windmill and these are illustrated in the pictures on this page. The **post mill** revolves round a central pillar. In this way it can be turned to make the best use of the wind. It is almost invariably built of wood. In the case of the **tower mill** only the rotating cap at the top moves round. The rest of the mill is, therefore, usually of the heavier stone or brick.

The windmill can only operate effectively when turned into the wind. The **fantail** introduced in the middle of the eighteenth century meant that the post mill or the tower mill cap was automatically turned by the wind itself into the wind!

WATERWHEELS

Waterwheels (which generate power by the use of water) can be divided into three main types depending on where the water strikes the blades of the wheel. **Overshot** wheels are those where the water is directed at the top of the wheel. **Breastshot** wheels are those where the water is directed lower down but still towards the upper half of the wheel. **Undershot** wheels are those where the water strikes the lower half of the wheel.

Overshot wheels are often powered by small fast streams taken along artificial gulleys or channels whilst undershot and breastshot wheels are usually to be found in larger, slower streams.

▲ **Lady Isabella water wheel, Isle of Man**

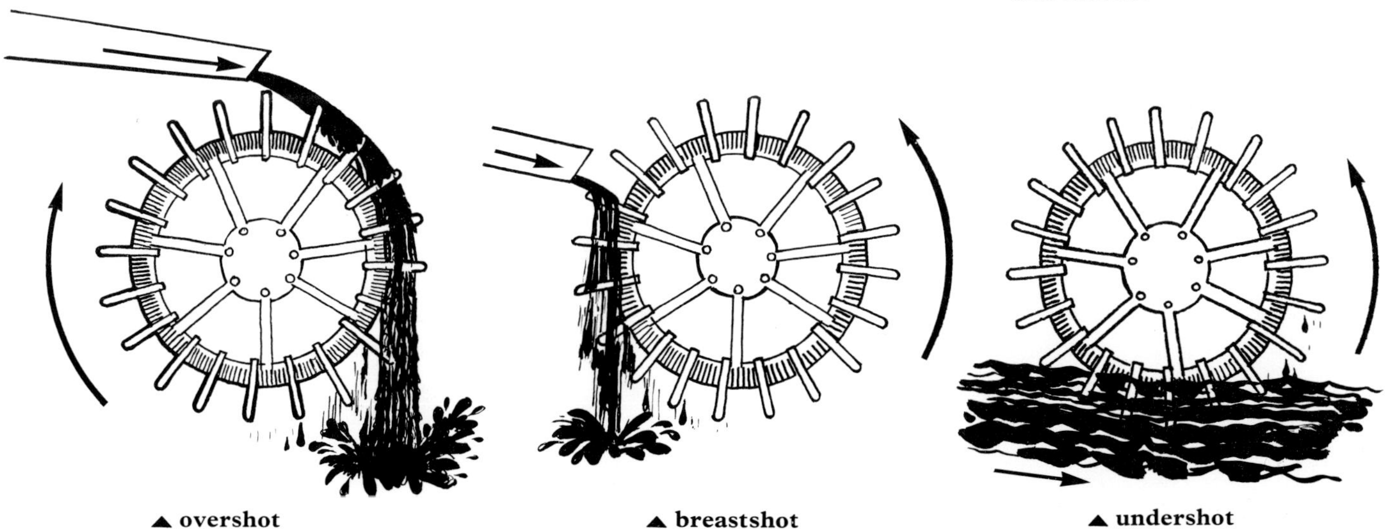

▲ **overshot** ▲ **breastshot** ▲ **undershot**

ENTERTAINMENTS: PAST AND PRESENT

Entertainments of the recent past can be seen in most towns. **Theatre** buildings have often passed through three or more stages within the space of twenty years or so. Some started as live theatre, were converted into **cinemas,** and with the advent of television were turned into **bingo halls** or **supermarkets.**

Earlier entertainments can sometimes be guessed from street names such as Cockpit Lane, the Bull Ring or The Chase (which recalls the days of hunting). Some places have specific sporting grounds or relics such as the **Butts** where archers practised with their longbows, the **Quintain** (or tilting post), as at Offham in Kent, which provided a target for tournament practice, or **bowling greens** such as the Tudor green at Melcombe Bingham in Dorset. **Cockpits** (for cock-fighting) or amphitheatres which could have been used as cockpits are sometimes in evidence in parts of the country.

◀ Victorian theatre

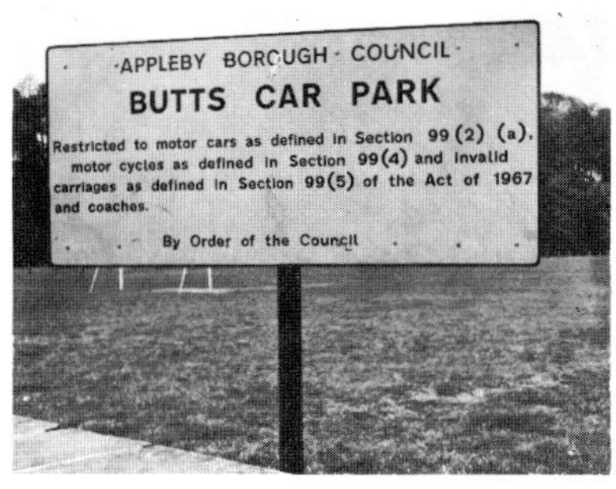

▲ street names

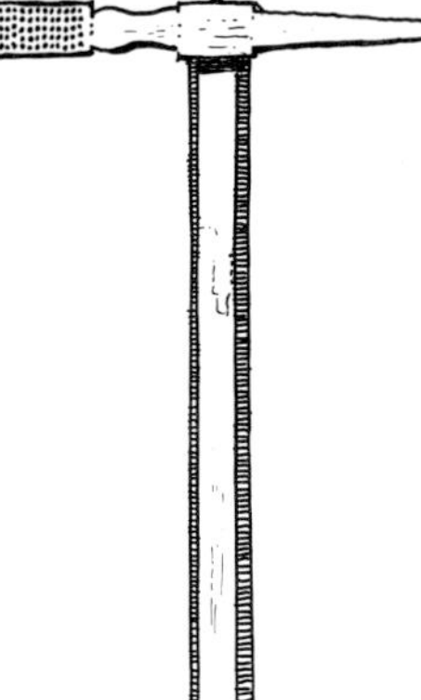

▲ quintain

▼ cockpit

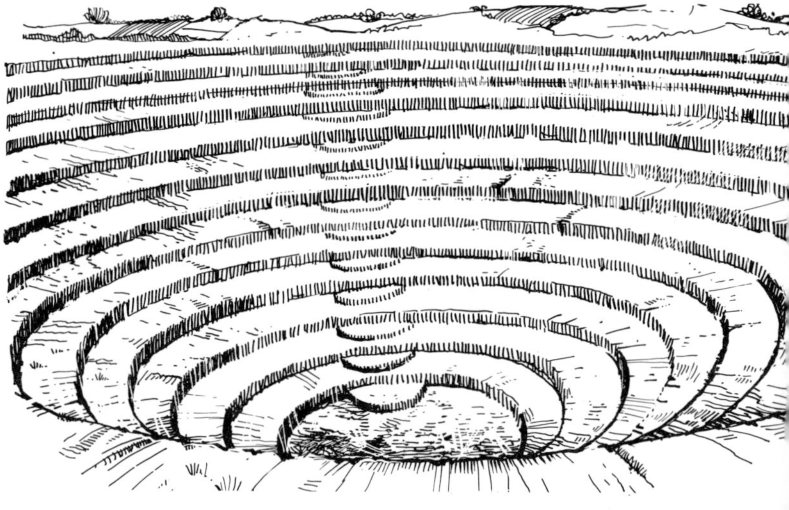

PUBLIC PARKS

Public parks were laid out in many British towns after 1848, to provide facilities for recreation and a touch of country in the rapidly built-up urban environment of the Victorian period. Public parks are often a treasure house of Victorian fashions and styles with **bandstands, fountains, statues, obelisks, follies, pavilions** and **gateways.**

MUSEUMS

Most places of any consequence at all maintain a **museum**. In almost every museum there are sections devoted to the lives of the local people at different periods of time. Some museums, in fact, are specially designed as "folk museums" whose function is simply to reflect the life and work of the people of the district. Museums are changing and no longer seem content to provide a passive exhibition. Working models, recordings and films often give a very lively presentation. Many museums have streets, shops, and houses realistically furnished so that to walk along them or through them is to take a step back into the past.

ON THE OUTSKIRTS OF A TOWN

On the fringe of any town there are **playing fields** and **suburban houses.** In the larger cities there are **airports, ring roads** and **zoos.** For many towns the outskirts conveniently house the **sewage works.**

AN AIRPORT

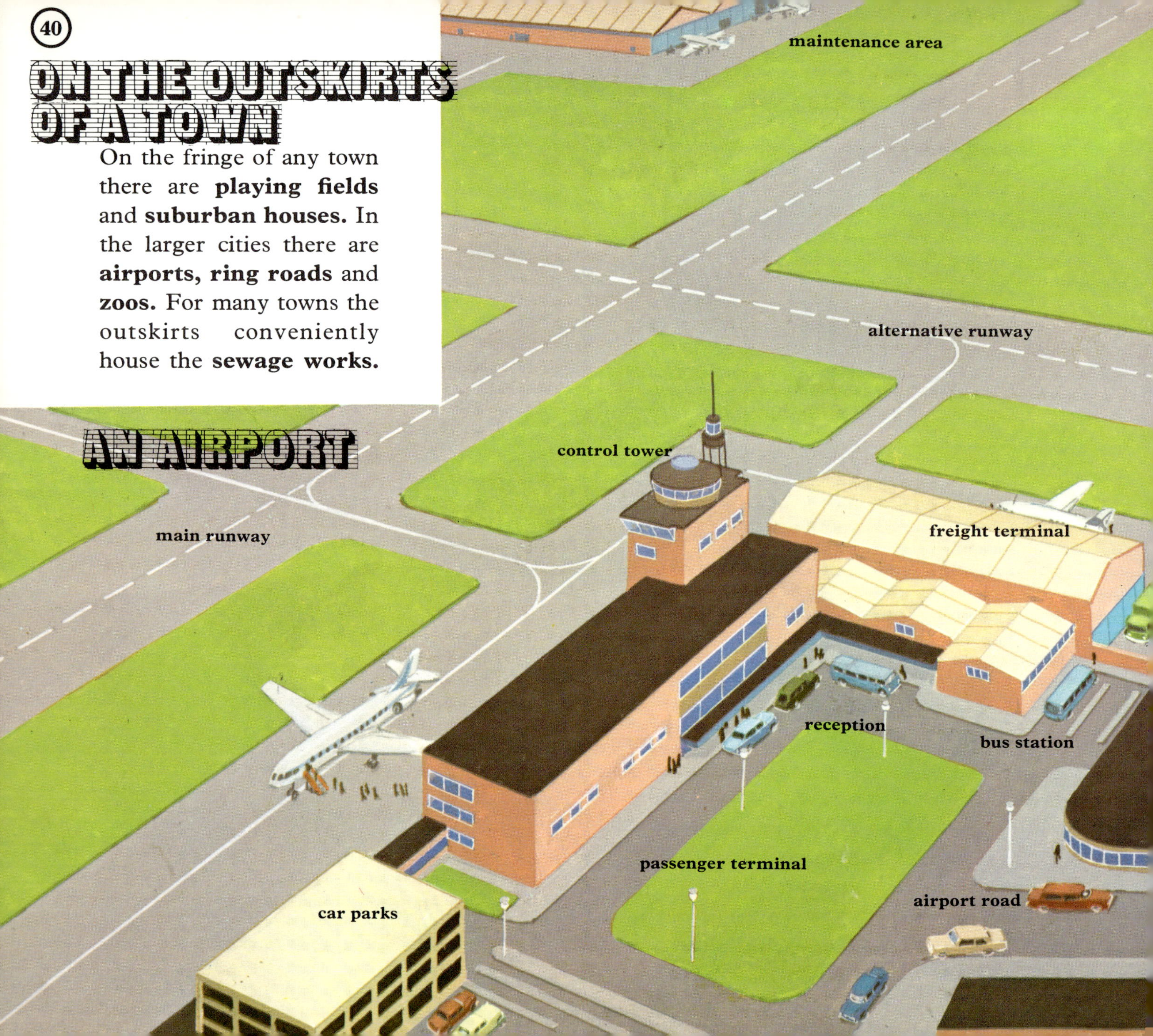

▲ suburbs

▲ ring road

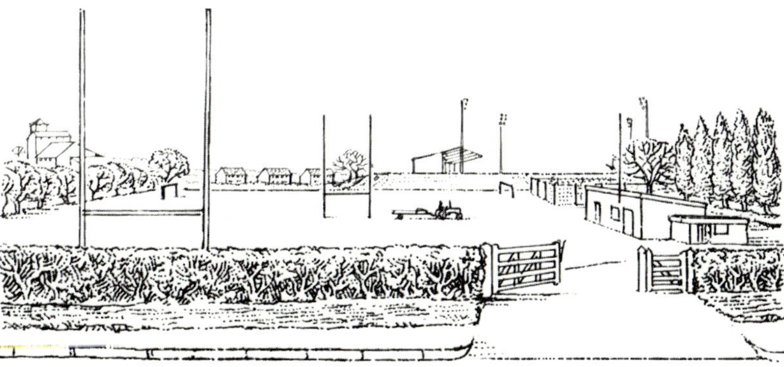

▲ sports ground

A SEWAGE WORKS

▲ sewage treatment works

The aim of any sewage works is to treat incoming raw sewage so that it can be safely discharged into a river or into the sea. In some sewage works the treatment is so successful that a glass of water taken after processing raw sewage can be purer than the town's water supply. Sewage plants differ from one another in the specific techniques used, but usually you can see **settling tanks** where much of the solids settle as sludge and **filter beds** of sand or gravel which purify the sewage until it is fit to be discharged through the **outfall pipes.**

WHEN TOWNS WERE ONCE FIELDS

▲ ridge and furrow

These illustrations show some of the ways in which a modern town can reveal something of the days when much of the town's area was farmland. **Street names** and the names of suburbs frequently recall fields, meadows and woods. Sometimes the telltale **ridge and furrow** of the medieval field system can be seen in a public park or on a common. Sometimes an old farm building in the town centre gives a clue to its size and extent in the medieval period. The oasthouse in Church Street, Saffron Walden, is a good example of this. A visit to the local library can often unearth old **town maps** showing the fields of the town a hundred years or so ago.

street names ▼

The Common

CHURCHFIELD ROAD

MEADOW STREET

Fieldsend Street

Mayfield Lane

Oakwood Lane

oasthouse in Saffron Walden ▼

▼ names of suburbs and districts

KINGSDOWN

MILLFIELD

NORRIS GREEN

HIGHFIELDS

BETHNAL GREEN

WOODSIDE

COUNTRY

PANORAMA: THE COUNTRYSIDE

white horse

stone circle

castle

Celtic fields

woodland

pond

hill fort

mansion
ruined abbey
church
inn
fence
gate
village green
stocks
farm
tumuli
hedge

VILLAGE TYPES

Villages often fall into one or other of the settlement types shown in the pictures on these pages.

Many villages are **linear** in shape and strung out along the course of a road, dyke or seafront. Many villages developed round **cross-roads**; some villages were sited within the meander of a **river.** Sometimes they were situated in a **valley** or in a gap between **hills.** Many villages grew up near a **spring** or **well** at the foot of an **escarpment** (see page 98). Many villages grew up round a **castle** or an **abbey.**

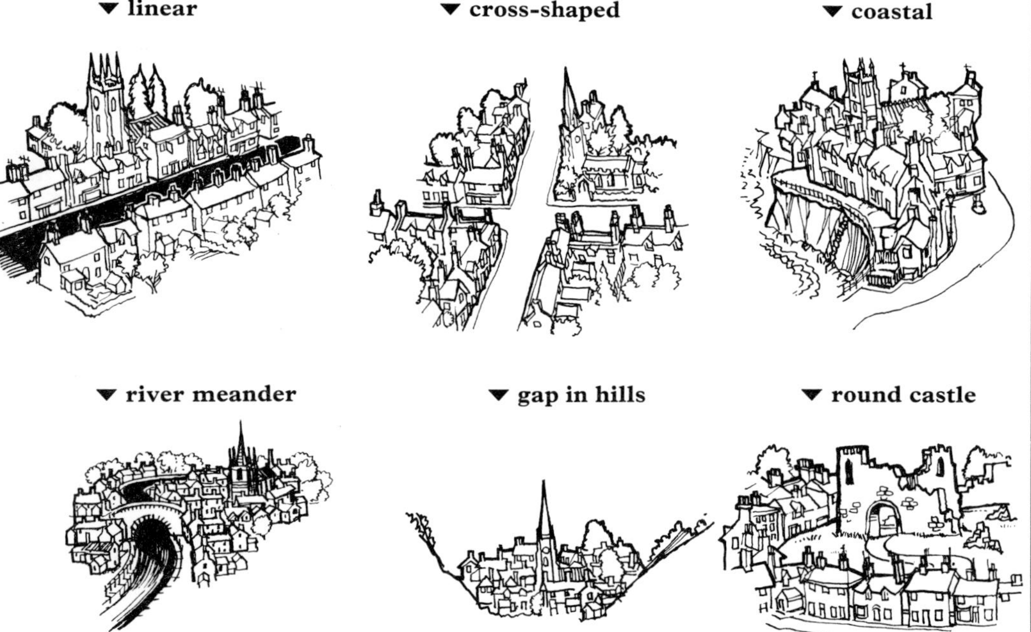

LOST VILLAGES

Whenever you see a ruined church and a manor house nearby standing in fields by themselves it is possible to suspect a "lost village"—a village which was deserted at some time in the past. Sometimes the "lost villages" can only be seen effectively from the air when hummocks and uneven ground throw shadows. A careful examination of an aerial photograph shows these to be the remains of old streets and houses.

WATER SUPPLY

In the days before mains water supply it was essential for a village to have a good reliable source of water. This usually meant **wells** and **pumps.** These tapped the water which lay below the surface of the land. A **trough** or **pond** for watering beasts and travellers' horses was also needed. Some village ponds probably date back to medieval times. Many of the troughs, wells and pumps were covered over by **shelters** so that villagers could use them in all weathers. In some villages you can see shelters erected over **cisterns.** A conduit or pipeline had been laid to bring water to a tank or cistern which acted as an artificial reservoir. In more sophisticated systems water was often piped to a **water tower** which also acted as a reservoir. To avoid the necessity of pumping the water to the houses the water tower was usually sited on a high point and built tall so that water was distributed by gravity.

village pond ▶

▼ pump

▲ horse trough

▼ covered well

▼ covered pump

▼ conduit

▼ water tower

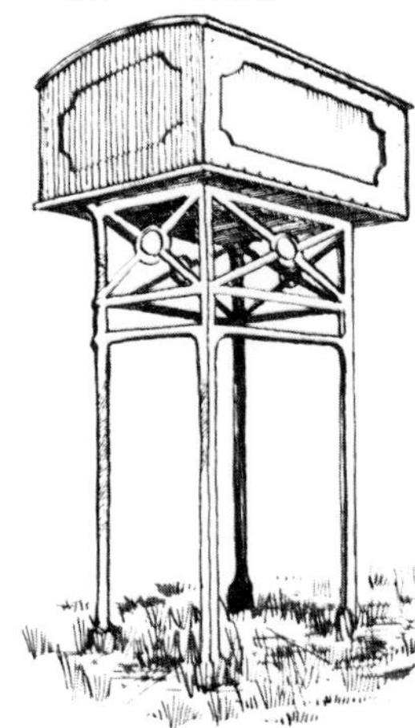

VILLAGE FEATURES

Cattle pounds were erected to house stray beasts and other animals.

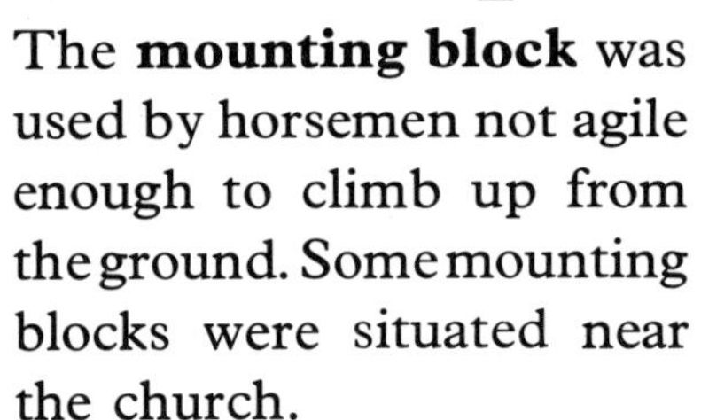

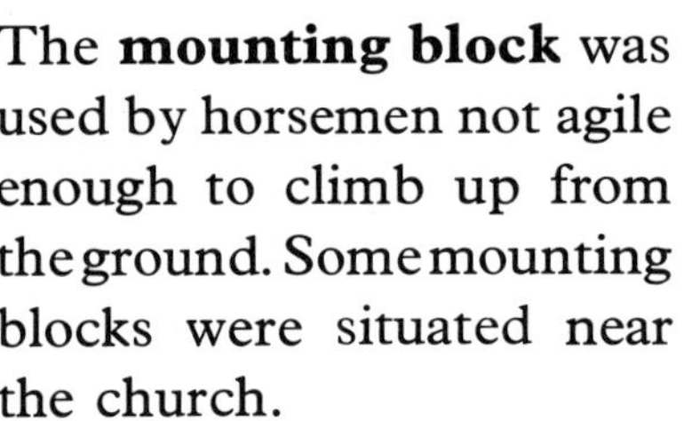

The **mounting block** was used by horsemen not agile enough to climb up from the ground. Some mounting blocks were situated near the church.

Dovecotes housed pigeons. Do not confuse them with the village **lock up** (see page 53).

Most villages have a **cross** in a central position. This is often a **memorial cross** erected after the First World War but other crosses are often seen as well as **market crosses** (see page 50). **Eleanor crosses** were erected in the thirteenth century to mark the places where the body of Queen Eleanor, wife of Edward I, lay each night on her last journey from Nottinghamshire to Westminster Abbey.

Eleanor cross

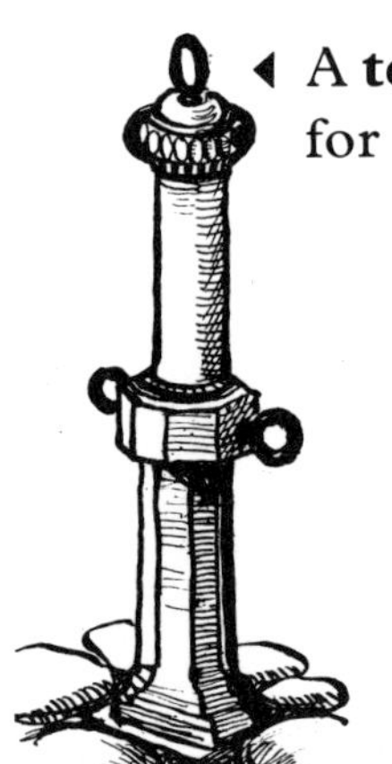

A **tethering post** was used for tying up one's horse.

Maypoles are a traditional feature of the village green.

Many villages had a **green** or **common** as their central focus. To many people a **village** is a settlement which has a **church,** a **post office,** a **school** and a **public house.** Settlements without these amenities are usually small and better described as **hamlets.**

MARKET FEATURES

Many large villages or small towns had the right to hold a **market. Market crosses** often mark the sites where these markets were held. Sometimes if the market was important or if it specialised in a particular trade or product, a **market hall** was erected. Sometimes a special **marketplace** was built. At King's Lynn in Norfolk two large squares have the names Saturday Marketplace and Tuesday Marketplace.

Many towns and villages still hold markets—often on the same days as in the Middle Ages many centuries ago.

domed ▲ market cross

▲ market halls ▼

stepped ▲ market crosses ▶

a seat or shelf on which to display market produce

eighteenth century market cross ▼

◀ covered markets ▶ to keep produce and traders dry

▲ sixteenth century market cross

▼ street sign

A CATTLE MARKET

Cattle markets are other interesting places to visit as you can see from this picture.

PUNISHMENTS OF THE PAST

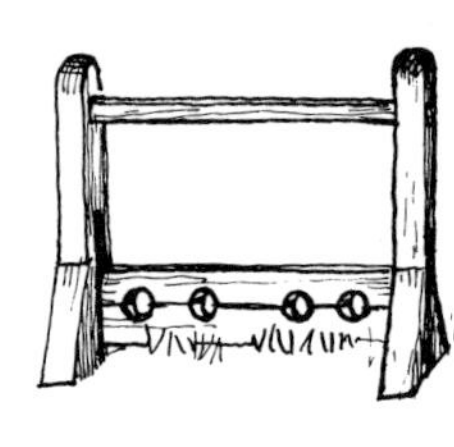

Stocks, where wrongdoers were put for punishment, are quite often found in villages, but **whipping posts** are less common. The stocks were last used in Britain a little over a century ago.

WHIP MA WHOP MA GATE

Street names such as those shown here often recall medieval methods of dealing with crime.

Gibbets or **gallows** remind us of a barbaric age when relatively minor crimes like stealing a loaf of bread could be punished with the death penalty.

Pillories are rare. The unfortunate criminal stood on the platform. His head went through the middle hole and his arms through the holes on either side. He was then pelted with mud, rotten apples and other missiles.

"Scolds"—women who nagged—were often ducked in a pond or stream by the villagers who kept a **"ducking stool"** handy for this purpose.

Lock-ups were the village prisons. They are often mistaken for dovecotes as they have a somewhat similar appearance (see page 48).

The **"jougs"** was a Scottish form of punishment—a collar of iron which was used to fasten a prisoner to a wall.

LOCAL STYLES OF BUILDING

The different styles of building that can be seen in different parts of the country are largely due to the differences in type and availability of suitable raw materials. In clay areas **bricks** could be made cheaply, and, not surprisingly, brick is the chief building material. In West Norfolk the houses are often built of **red sandstone,** Aberdeen is the **granite** city, while Cotswold village houses are often built of the local **limestone.** In the **chalk** areas it is not uncommon to find houses and other buildings in which **flints** have played a major part in the raw materials used. The industrial towns of Yorkshire have houses built of **millstone grit**—a tough sandstone often discoloured by soot and smoke. In these pictures you can see some of these distinctive regional styles of building.

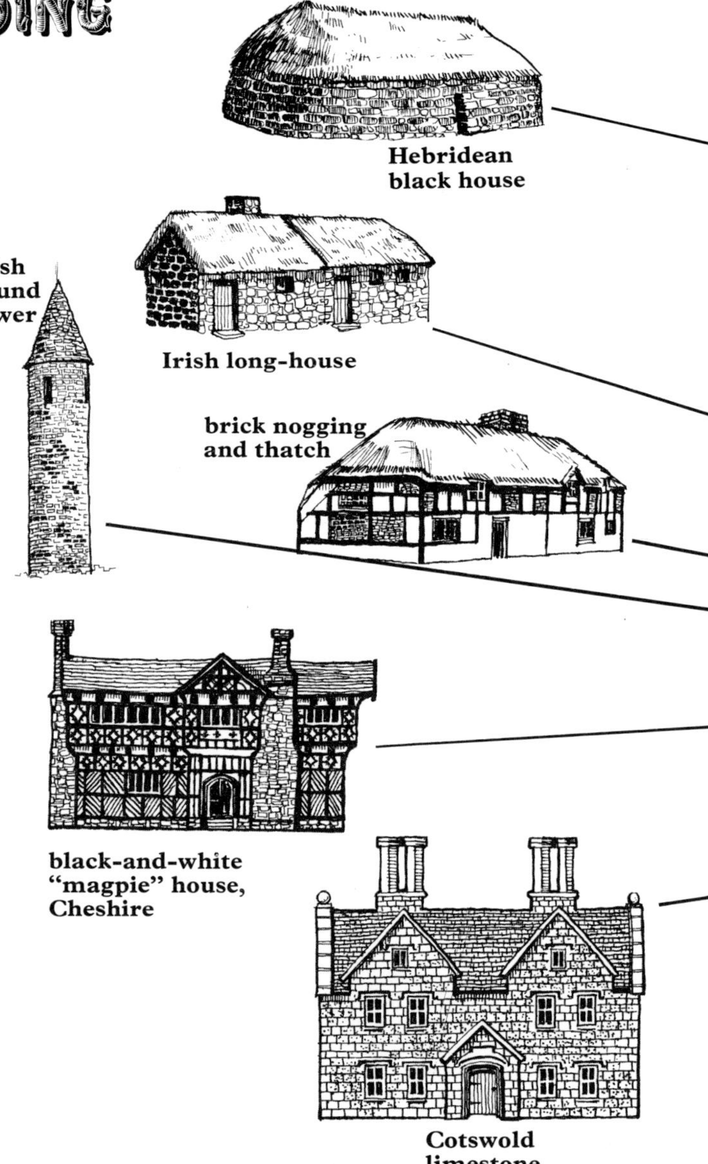

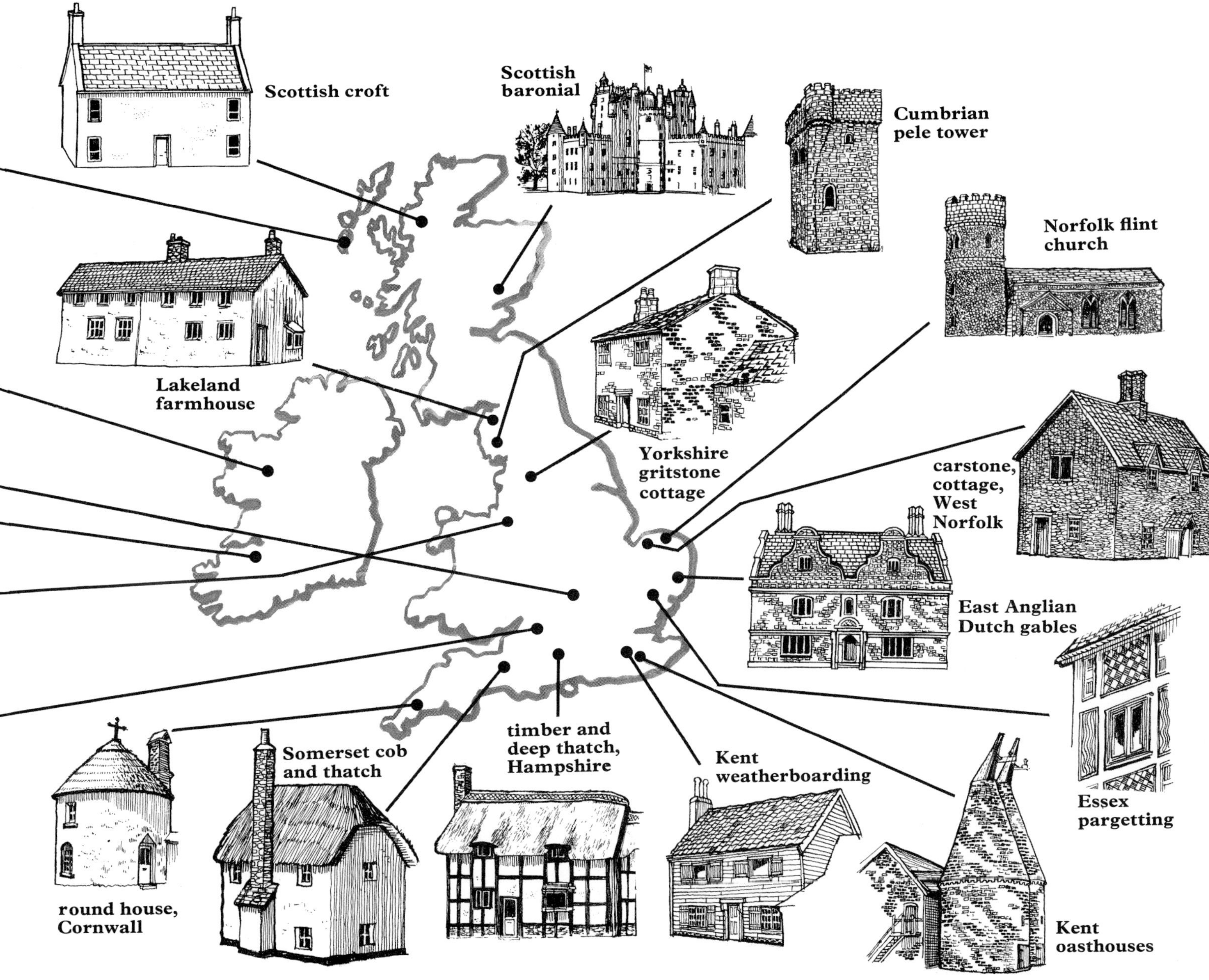
Scottish croft
Scottish baronial
Cumbrian pele tower
Norfolk flint church
Lakeland farmhouse
Yorkshire gritstone cottage
carstone, cottage, West Norfolk
East Anglian Dutch gables
Essex pargetting
Kent oasthouses
Kent weatherboarding
timber and deep thatch, Hampshire
Somerset cob and thatch
round house, Cornwall

METHODS OF CONSTRUCTION: STONEWORK

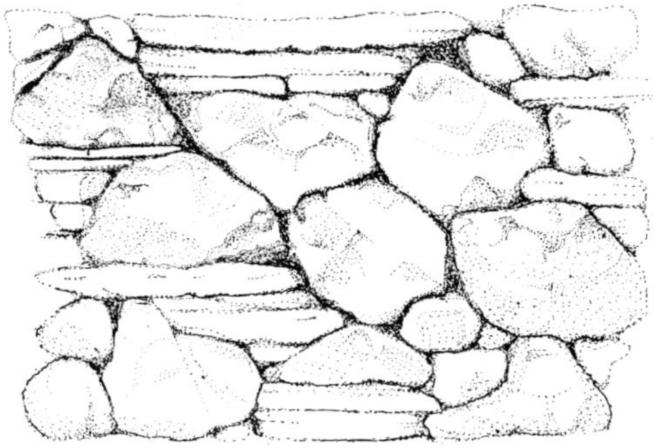

▲ uncoursed (irregular blocks)

▲ coursed (regular layers)

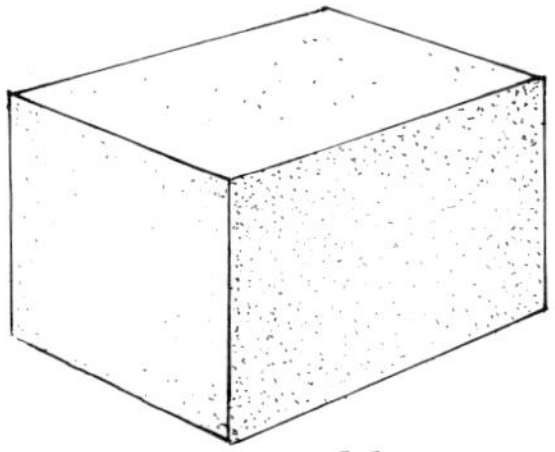

▲ ashlar—
even-sized
stones cut
to give smooth
finish

▼ dry (no cement)

corner stones
of large
ashlar blocks

small
pebbles

▲ pointed (embedded in mortar or cement)

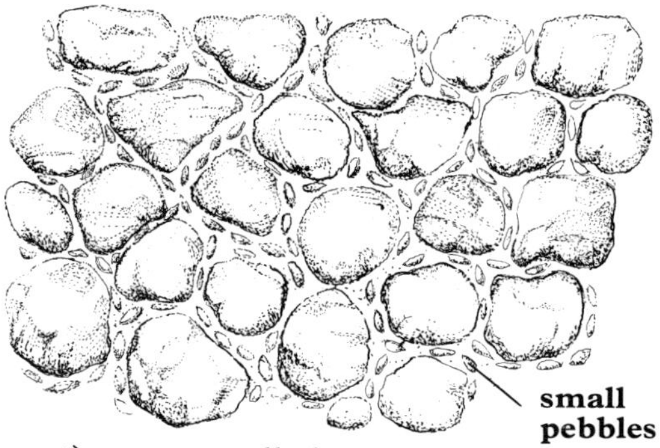

▲ galleting

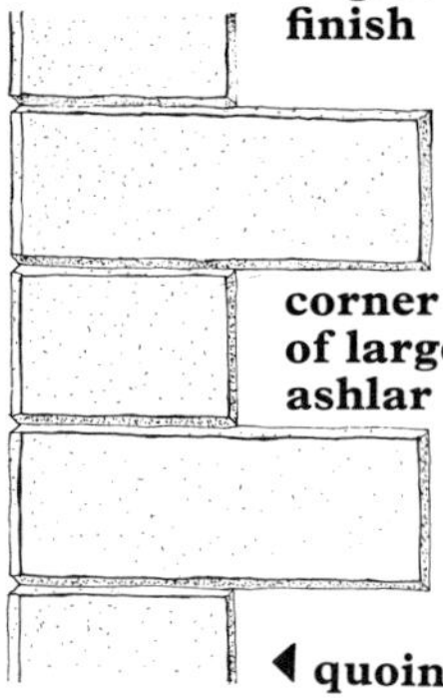

◀ quoins

▼ gritstone

▲ cobbles

▼ Cotswold limestone

▲ pebbles

▼ Lake District slate

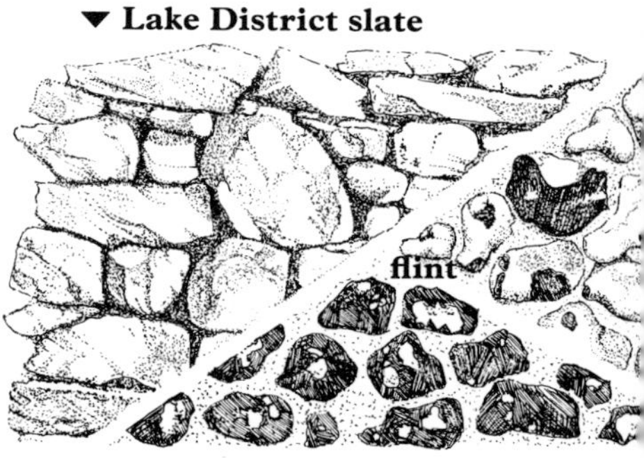

▲ knapped flint

header stretcher

BRICKWORK

▼ English bond ▼ Flemish bond ▼ Norman herringbone ▼ heading bond

TIMBERWORK

The main types of house built with a **timber frame** are shown here—the **cruck-framed cottage** and the **box-framed house.** The timber frames formed the structures and some other building material was then used for the walls. The building material did not need to be strong since the timber structure took the strain. The commonest type of walling for the houses of ordinary people was called **"wattle and daub".** This was formed from a clay mixture which was "daubed" on to a woven framework of willow wands or withies. It was **plastered** and then **whitewashed.** For this reason many half-timbered cottages give a **black and white** effect. In many houses the wattle and daub was later replaced by **"brick nogging"** which was a brick wall between the timbers, using frequently "herring bone" brickwork.

studs (timber posts)

jetty (over hanging floor joists)

▲ cruck-framed ▼

▲ box-framed ▼

▼ wattle and daub

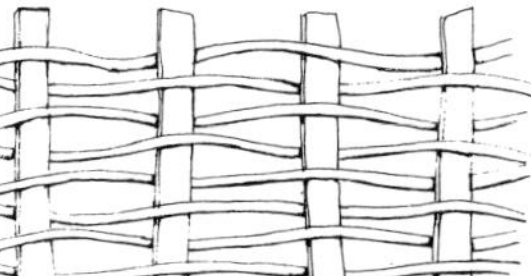

1. wattles

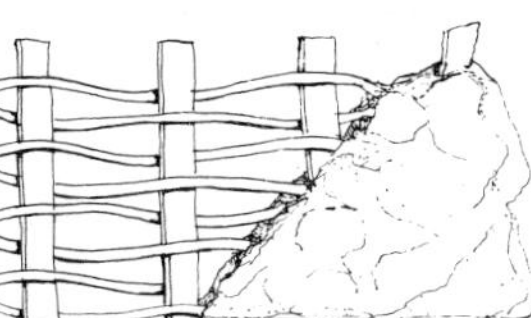

2. daubed with clay

3. plastered

4. whitewashed

▼ brick nogging

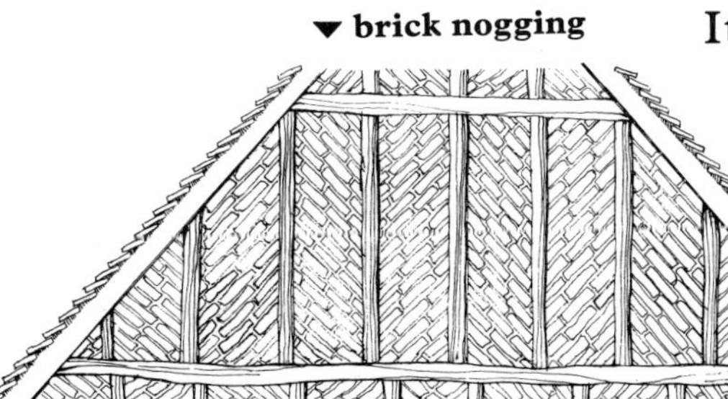

METHODS OF CONSTRUCTION: WALLS

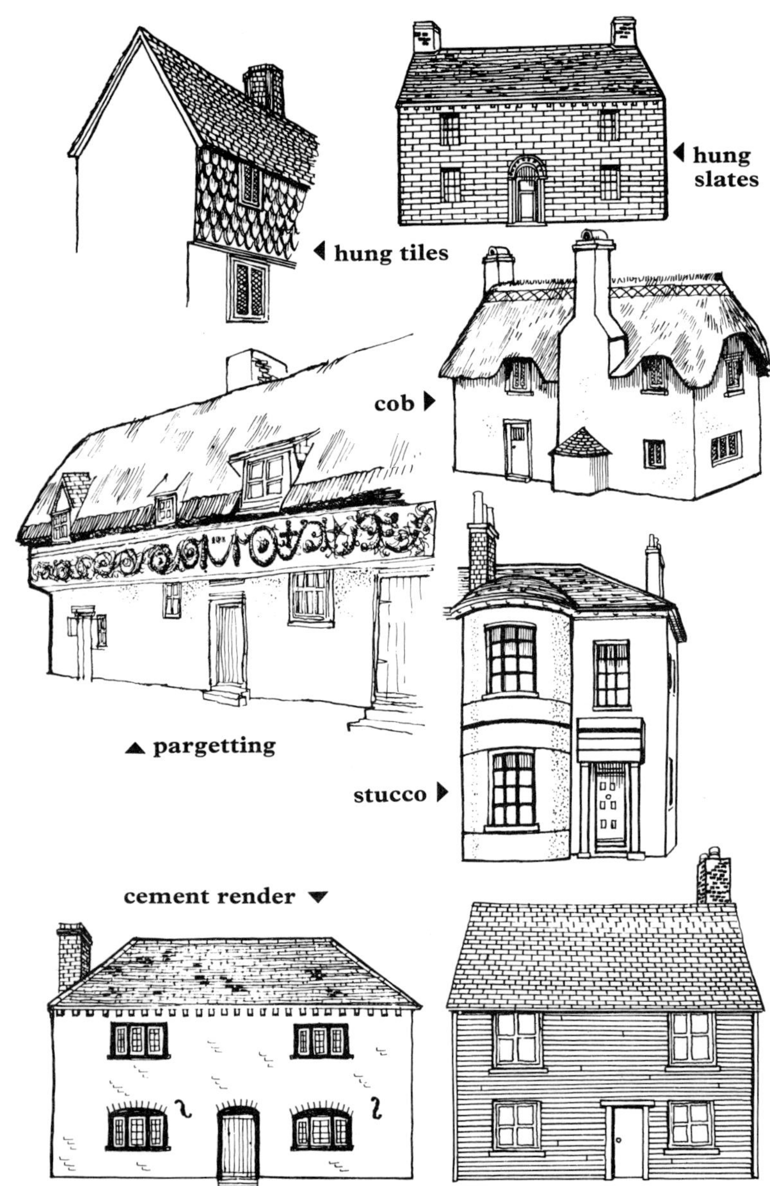

The walls of a house have to be waterproof and able to insulate the interior so that it is warm in winter and cool in summer. The walls of a house can also be a decorative feature whether through the texture and colour of the covering materials or by their design. In some parts of the country you can find houses where parts of the walls are hung with **tiles** or **slates.** These were more effective than wattle and daub and, in fact, are still rated highly as wall coverings. In the rural areas of the south-west houses were often made with **cob** which is a mixture of clay, sand, gravel, straw and cow-hair or horse-hair. In Essex and other parts of East Anglia decorated plaster covers the walls of many houses. This decorated plaster is known as **pargetting** and often features designs with raised or etched patterns. Much of it dates back to the seventeenth and early eighteenth centuries. In many areas horizontal timber planks are used in the style known as **weather boarding** or **clap boarding.** This usually dates from the eighteenth century. **Cement render** and **stucco** are other forms of wall covering.

ROOFS

On this page you can see some of the main types of roofing material. Details of the different types of roof structure can be seen on pages 26-27.

Thatch is usually either reed or straw and it is ▶ still relatively common as a roof covering in certain rural areas (for example, north Essex). Thatched roofs are good insulators. **Reed thatch** lasts up to three times the length of **straw thatch.**

When **slates** were originally used for roofing ▶ it was only economic to use them on houses relatively close to the slate quarries.

Stone or **clay tiles** date from the seventeenth ▶ century and later, and are the most common type of roof covering.

The S-shaped **pantiles** are among the more ▶ attractive roof coverings.

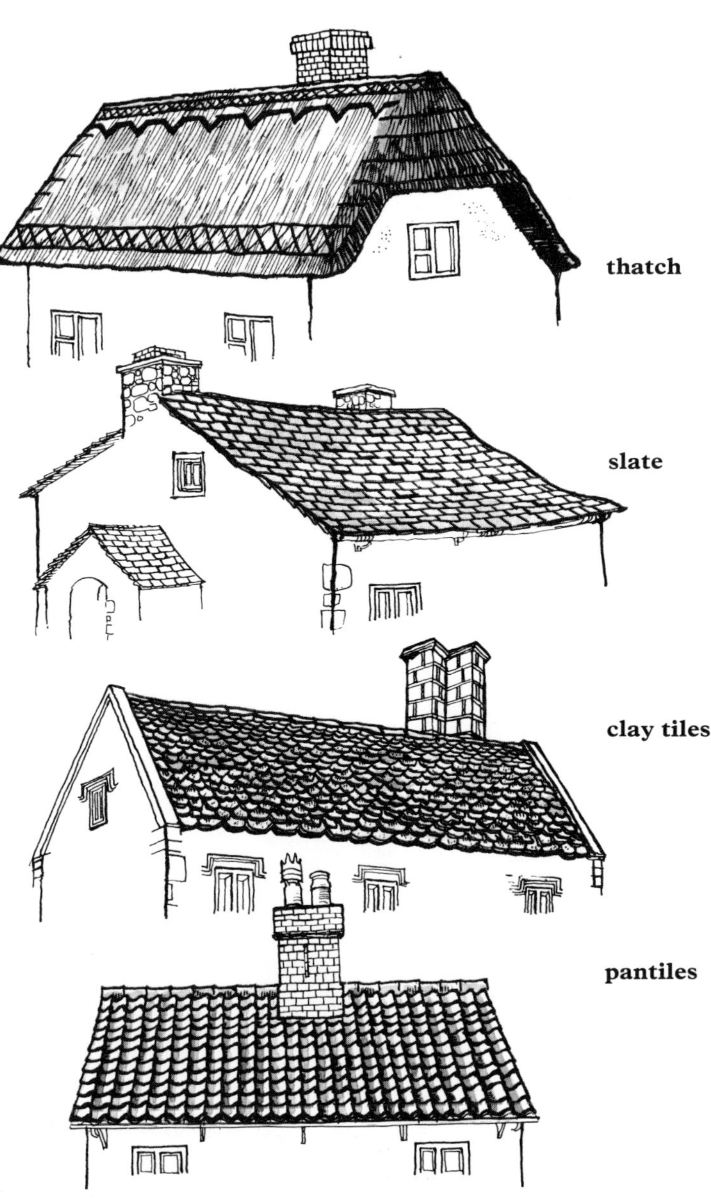

CHURCHES

Churches can be classified in many different ways; according to their age and style (see pages 62 and 63); according to their building materials (**stone, timber, flint, brick, concrete**); according to their shape and format (**square** and **round towers, steeples,** plain **meeting rooms, round buildings**); according to their religious denomination; according to their origin (**wool churches** built by the profits of the medieval woollen industry, Victorian **chapels** built to serve the needs of a growing population in the industrial revolution).

Perpendicular church with spire ▶

▲ Saxon tower

▲ Norman church

flint church ▶

▼ timber church

eighteenth century church ▶

▼ Perpendicular wool church

▲ Victorian chapel

▲ Early English church with detached tower

Lakeland ▶
stone church

modern cathedral ▶

◀ Crusader church

CHURCH STYLES

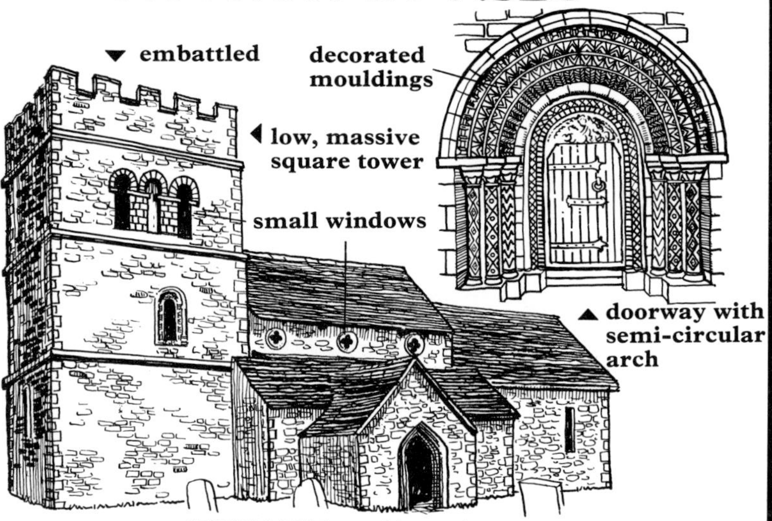

NORMAN (c. 1066-1200)

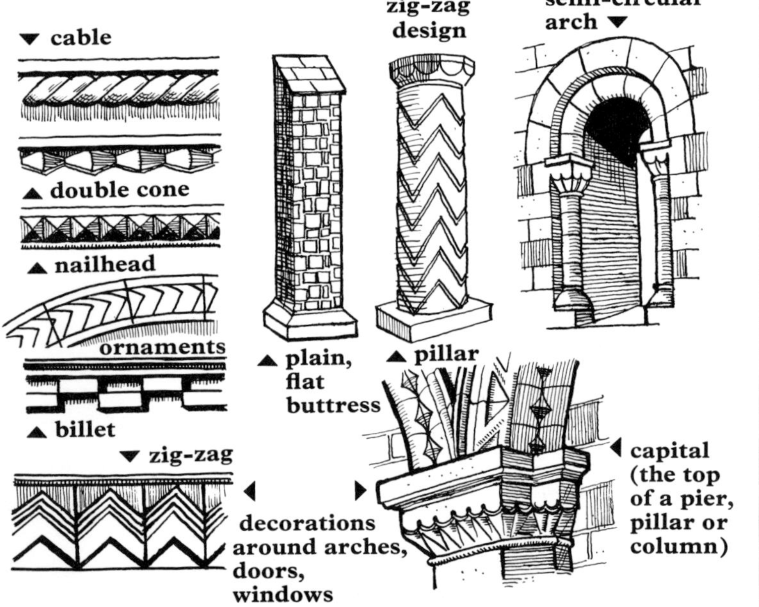

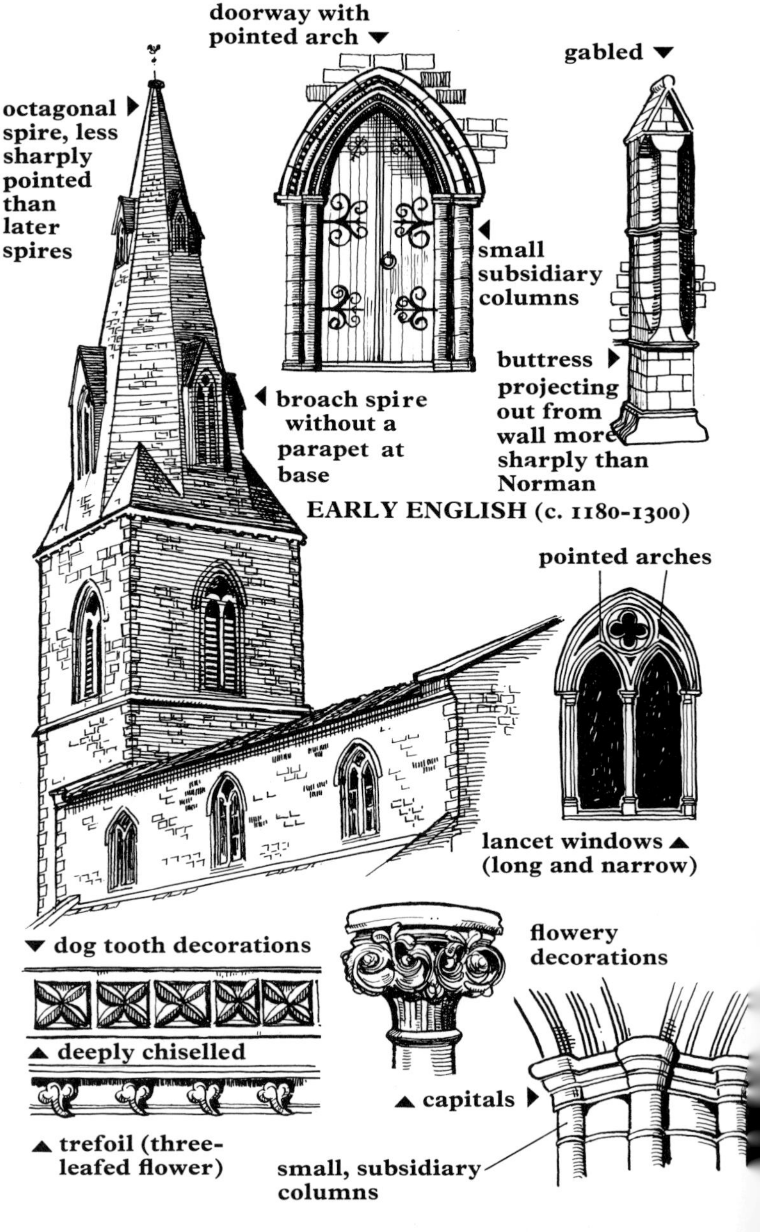

octagonal spire, less sharply pointed than later spires

doorway with pointed arch

gabled

small subsidiary columns

buttress projecting out from wall more sharply than Norman

broach spire without a parapet at base

EARLY ENGLISH (c. 1180-1300)

pointed arches

lancet windows (long and narrow)

dog tooth decorations

deeply chiselled

trefoil (three-leafed flower)

flowery decorations

capitals

small, subsidiary columns

fussy decoration (crockets)

sharply pointed spire

parapet with prominent decorated pinnacles

many narrow mouldings

▲ wider archway

DECORATED (c. 1280-1380)

curvilinear or flowing tracery (emphasis on circles and curves)

▲ crockets ▼

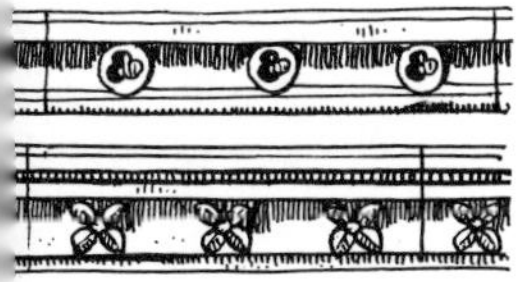

▼ ball flower

▲ tablet flower

elaborate carved capital

▲ tall "perpendicular" tower

PERPENDICULAR (c. 1350-1550)

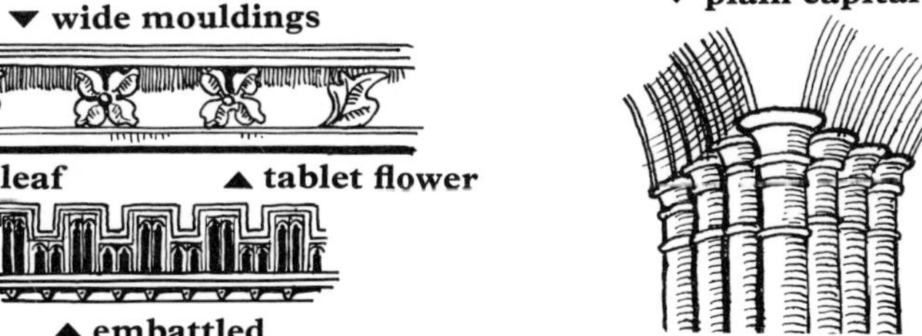

▲ memorial stone to a craftsman

▲ figure on tomb

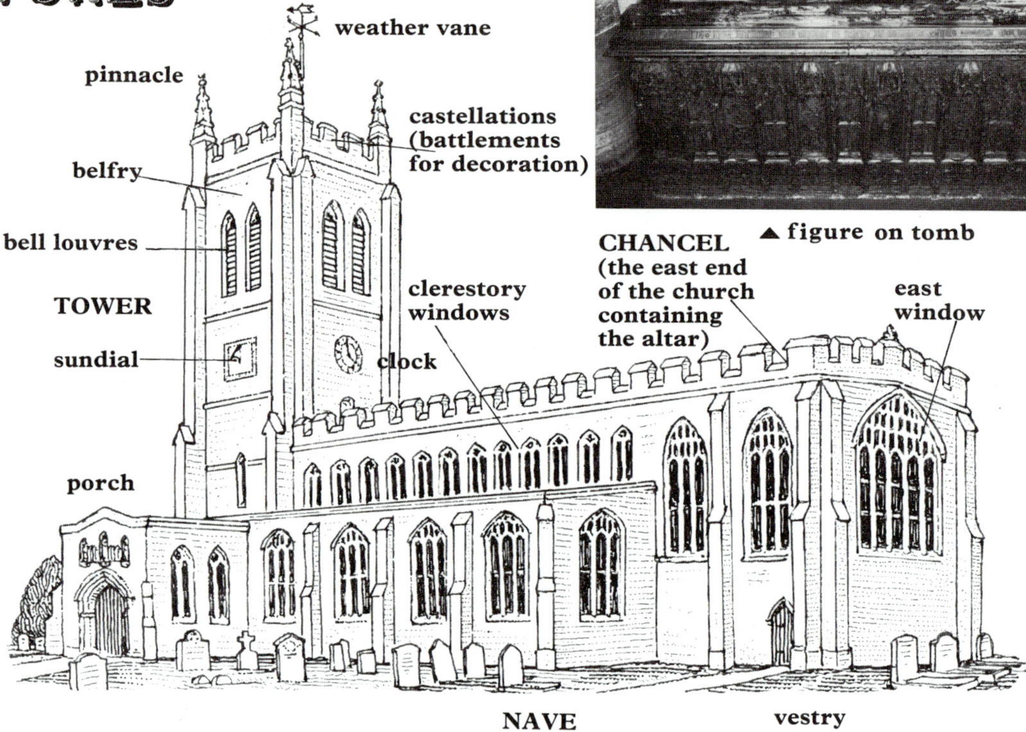

▲ stained glass

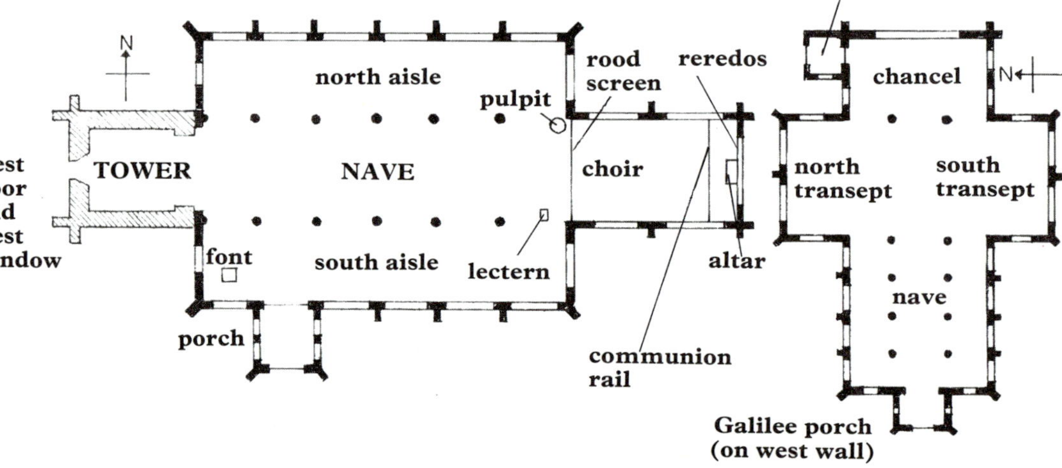

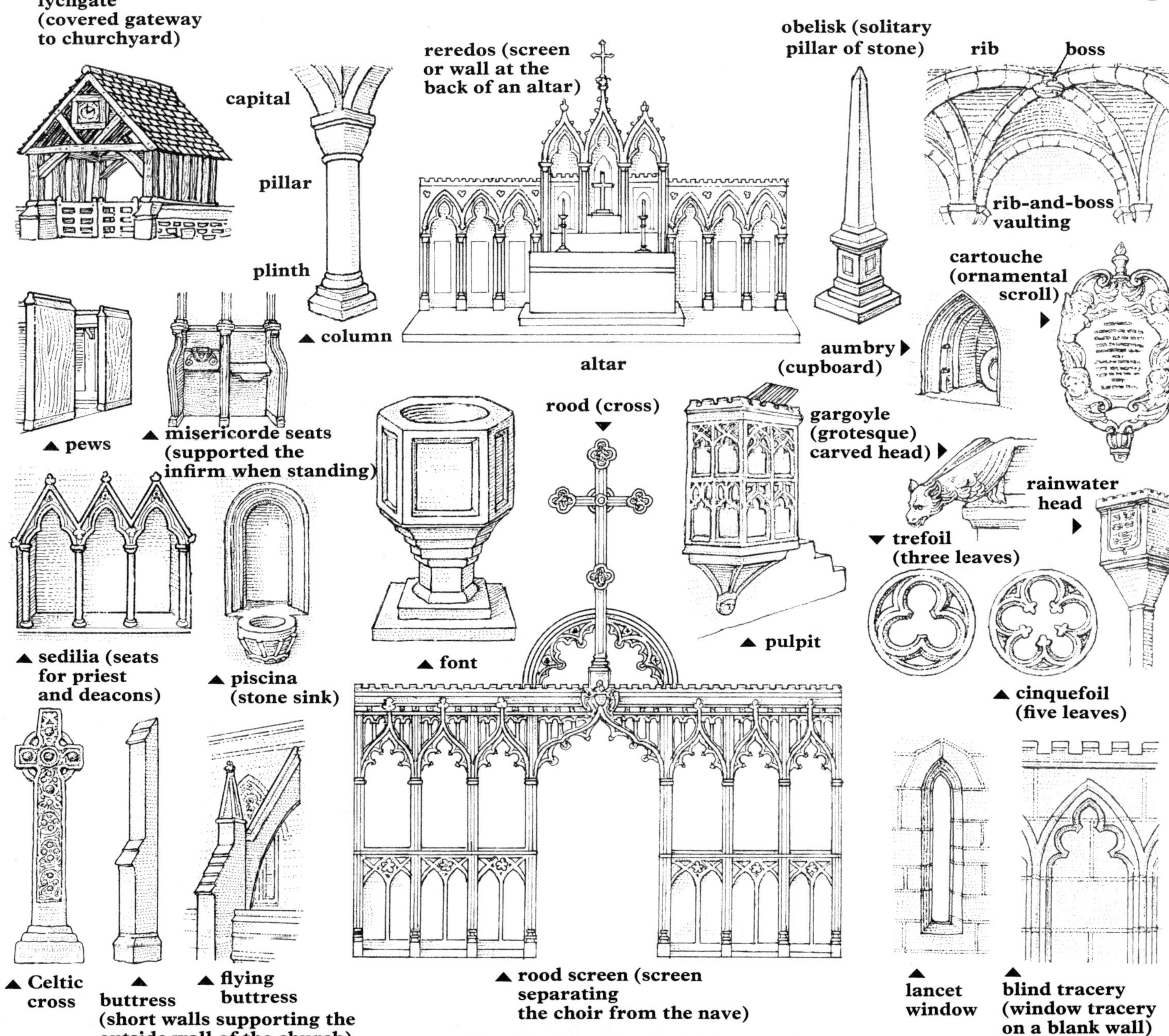
lychgate
(covered gateway
to churchyard)
capital
pillar
plinth
▲ column
reredos (screen
or wall at the
back of an altar)
altar
obelisk (solitary
pillar of stone)
rib
boss
rib-and-boss
vaulting
cartouche
(ornamental
scroll) ▶
aumbry ▶
(cupboard)
▲ pews
▲ misericorde seats
(supported the
infirm when standing)
rood (cross)
gargoyle
(grotesque)
carved head) ▶
rainwater
head ▶
▼ trefoil
(three leaves)
▲ cinquefoil
(five leaves)
▲ sedilia (seats
for priest
and deacons)
▲ piscina
(stone sink)
▲ font
▲ pulpit
▲ Celtic
cross
▲
buttress
▲ flying
buttress
(short walls supporting the
outside wall of the church)
▲ rood screen (screen
separating
the choir from the nave)
▲
lancet
window
▲
blind tracery
(window tracery
on a blank wall)

COUNTRY MANSIONS

avenue
planted trees
ornamental lake
dammed stream
urn
stables
summer house or pavilion
bridge
fountain
terrace
folly
pergola
formal garden
statue
maze
tropical house

▲ ha ha

The important building styles and architectural features to be seen when visiting a country mansion can be referred to on pages 19 to 29. The **gardens** of the mansion are often of equal interest. Many gardens or parks were designed by the great landscape gardeners of the eighteenth century such as Capability Brown. They created gardens with many artificial features. Trees and sometimes cottages were removed in order to give good views from the windows of the mansion. Great **avenues** were landscaped and planted with trees to give an impressive sweep up to the front of a house. **Ornamental lakes, dammed streams, fountains, bridges** and **terraces** are common features. The various garden buildings, such as the different types of **summerhouse,** are other interesting features to visit. Some are designed like **Greek temples,** some as **observatories** or **pavilions**; some were designed to catch a view and were even built on artificial hills for this purpose. They are variously known as **belvederes, gazebos** and **prospect towers.** The **hedges** are usually elaborately cut and trained to form shapes and animals. The art of hedge-shaping is known as **topiary.** The garden buildings are sometimes designed to

▲ **folly**

▲ **maze**

look like ruins. They are often described as being **sham ruins** or **follies**. In some gardens there are **mazes**. One of the most interesting features to be seen is the **ha ha.** This was a fence erected at the bottom of a ditch. In this way it acted as a fence and kept cattle and other beasts from straying on to the formal gardens and at the same time it did not spoil the view from the house.

▼ **gothic garden pavilion**

▼ **topiary**

AN ABBEY

In this diagram you can see a typical abbey as it might have looked over six hundred years ago. Nowadays most of the old monasteries are in ruins, having been pillaged and destroyed in the middle of the sixteenth century. A guide book is usually necessary to help identify the different parts of the abbey, for in many cases only the foundations of the walls remain. Some of the great abbeys, however, are sufficiently intact for the visitor to get a very good idea of how the monastery was laid out.

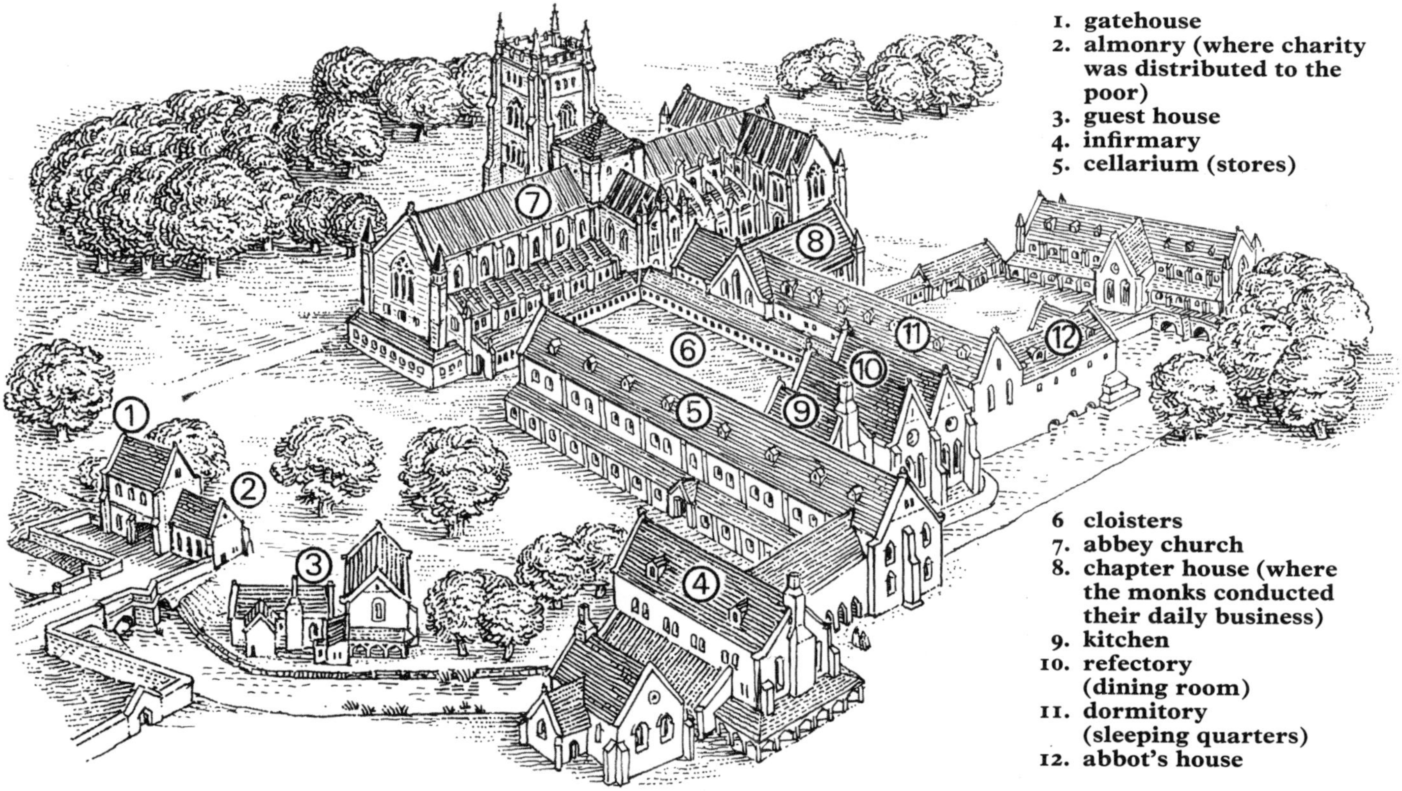

1. gatehouse
2. almonry (where charity was distributed to the poor)
3. guest house
4. infirmary
5. cellarium (stores)

6 cloisters
7. abbey church
8. chapter house (where the monks conducted their daily business)
9. kitchen
10. refectory (dining room)
11. dormitory (sleeping quarters)
12. abbot's house

FEATURES OF AN ABBEY

▲ The **church** was the focal point of a monk's life, for his day was regularly punctuated by church services, starting with one in the early hours of the morning and culminating with one late at night. Many abbey churches have the grandeur and proportions of a cathedral.

The **dormitory (or dorter)** was where the monks slept. The monasteries were surprisingly advanced for the period of time when they flourished. There were toilet basins (often close to the refectory) and there were lavatories (the **reredorter)**. This was the monastic toilet block. The monks used cubicles, and sewage emptied direct into a stream or drain.

dormitory

◀ The **chapter house** was the business centre of the abbey. The day's business was conducted here at about 10.00 a.m.

The **cloisters** formed a square or quadrangle where the monks could go for recreation or for thought. The square lawn was surrounded by an open corridor on all four sides. ▼

The **refectory** was the dining room of the monastery and here the monks filed in after their main church service of the day at 11.00 a.m. ▼

CASTLES

Castles are to be found in most parts of the British Isles. Most of them date back to the period from the Norman Conquest in 1066 to the start of the fourteenth century. They usually occupy prominent sites. Many are in ruins but even so their ground plan often shows that they follow a typical design (such as the one shown on page 72).

Motte and bailey

These were the earliest Norman castles and consisted of a **ditch,** a **mound,** a wooden **fort** on top and a **fence** leading down the hill enclosing an area known as the **bailey.** The wooden buildings have long since disappeared but sometimes ◀ the hills or "mottes" can be seen.

▲

Keeps

When the Normans had established a foothold in England, they built permanent castles of **stone.** These usually featured a strong central **keep** surrounded by walls with battlements.

Curtain walls

Later castles were designed ▶ with strong **curtain walls** in which all the principal rooms of the castle were incorporated, usually in strong **towers.** Sometimes a double circle of walls formed the **concentric castle.**

Fortified manor houses

In the fourteenth and fifteenth centuries some nobles built fortified manor houses. These were strong enough to protect the occupants against minor raids and yet offered greater comfort than the castle. In East Anglia in particular, many houses were surrounded by **moats** in the fourteenth, fifteenth and sixteenth centuries.

Tudor forts

These were built by Henry VIII to defend the southern coast of England against foreign invasion by sea. They were specifically designed as artillery forts with wide **platforms** to carry the guns.

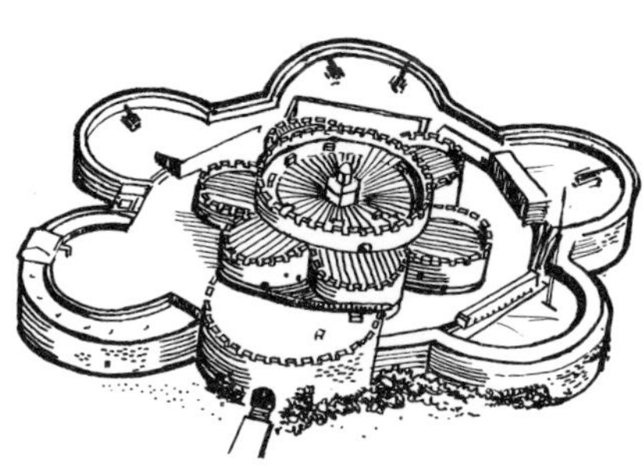

Scottish baronial castles

In Scotland several different types of castle can be seen from fortified farm houses to forbidding baronial strongholds. These Scottish castles have a distinctive architectural style of their own much copied by later architects. They frequently feature **towers** or **turrets** surmounted by a **cone.** Many resemble the chateaus of France or the castles of Germany.

Pele towers

These were strong fortified towers built, particularly in the borderlands of England and Scotland, against bands of marauders crossing the border and harassing the occupants.

CASTLE FEATURES

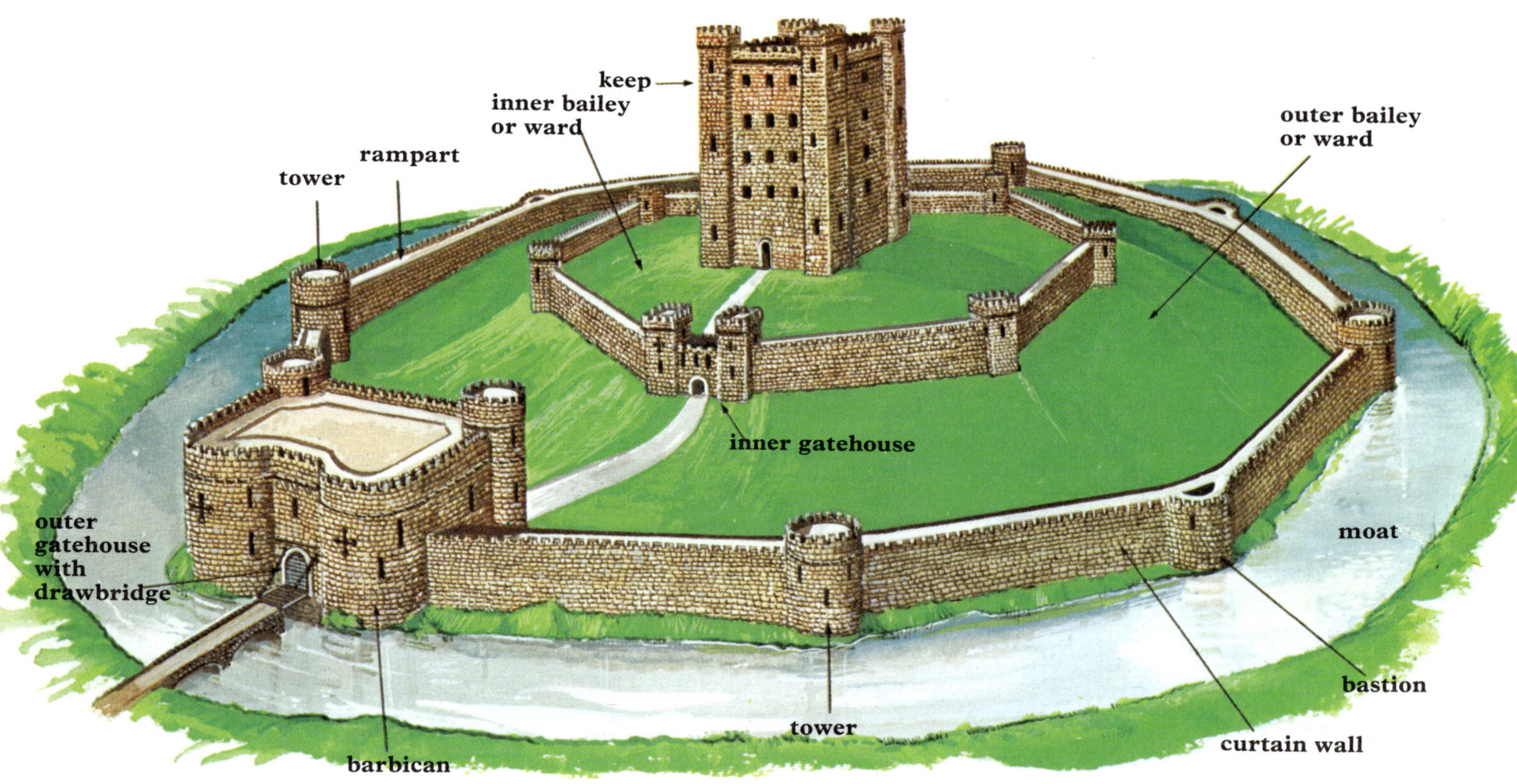

The **portcullis** was a door with iron or wooden bars which slid in grooves. It was usually kept suspended in the **gatehouse,** but was let down against invaders.

The **barbican** was an outer defence which could be used to defend the **drawbridge.** This was a bridge which could be raised or lowered across the **moat.**

Toilets were set within the thick walls and were known as **garderobes.** Meals were eaten in the **great hall** of the castle. Castle **kitchens, wells** and **granaries** can usually be located.

▲ arrow loops

Machiolations were holes let into the roof or in projections (**corbels**) from the battlements. They allowed missiles to be hurled down on the heads of attacking soldiers.

Arrow loops were holes let into the walls from which bowmen could pick off enemy soldiers. The long slits were for longbowmen. Horizontal slits were designed for archers using cross bows.

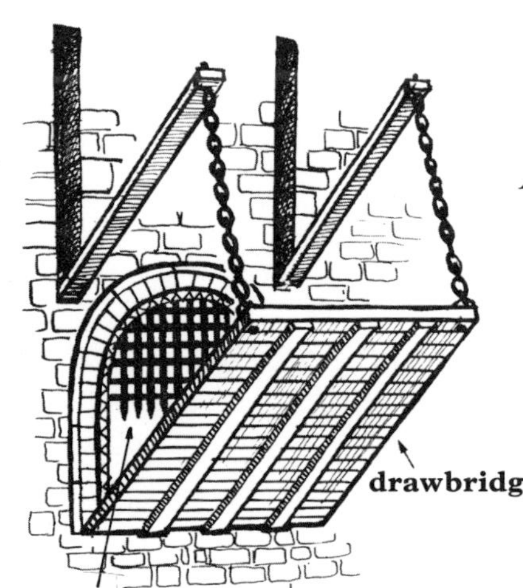

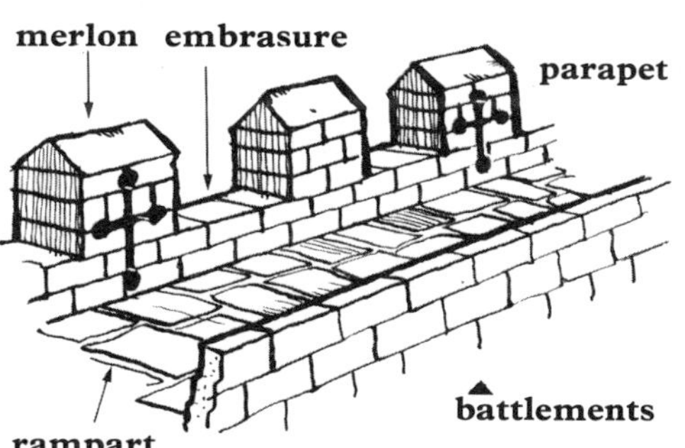

▲ battlements

▲ gatehouse

Bartizans were small overhanging **turrets** projecting from the corners of towers or from the **parapet.** ▶

A FARM

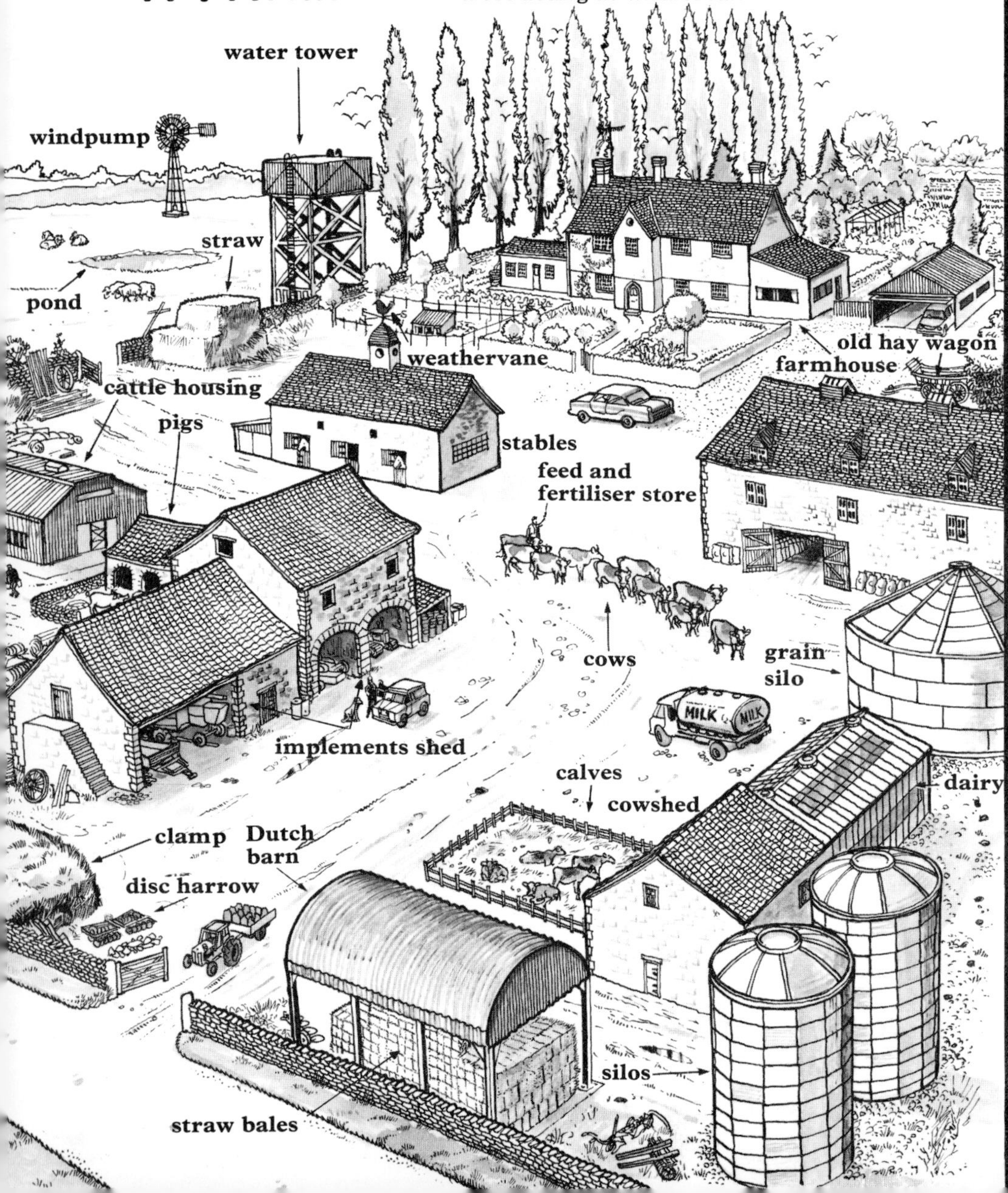

trees acting as windbreak
water tower
windpump
straw
pond
weathervane
old hay wagon
farmhouse
cattle housing
pigs
stables
feed and fertiliser store
cows
grain silo
implements shed
calves
cowshed
dairy
clamp
Dutch barn
disc harrow
silos
straw bales

FARMHOUSES

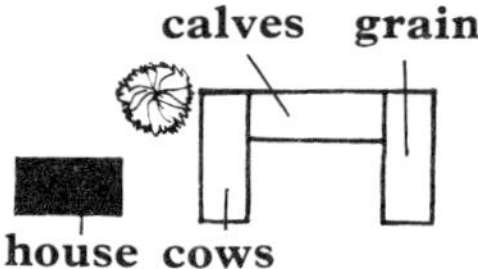

▲ detached from farm buildings

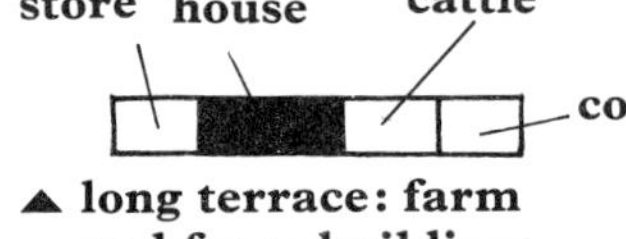

▲ long terrace: farm and farm buildings

▼ courtyard

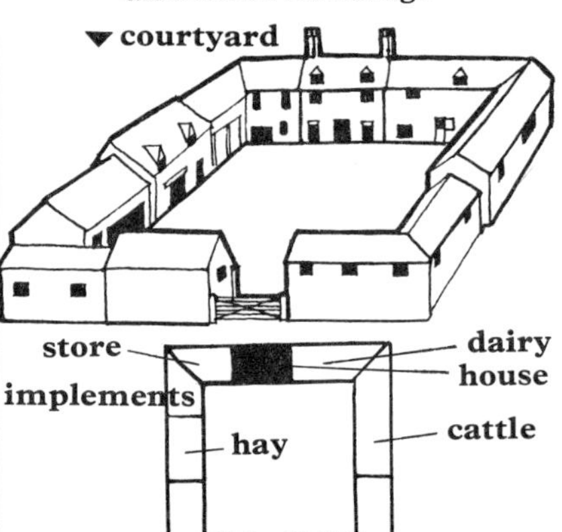

FARM IMPLEMENTS

Ploughs dig up the land. ▶ The ploughshares cut **furrows** which turn the land over. Some ploughs have several **blades** or **ploughshares.**

Harrows, cultivators and ▶ **discs** chop up the furrows and clods of soil and break the land down to provide a fine soil ready for sowing.

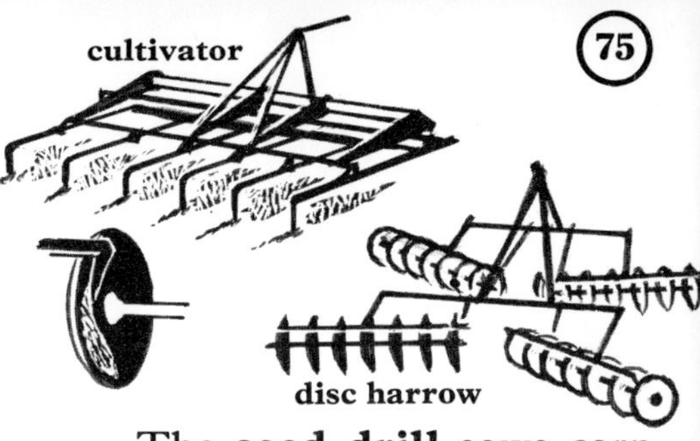

The **seed drill** sows corn seed in rows. ▼

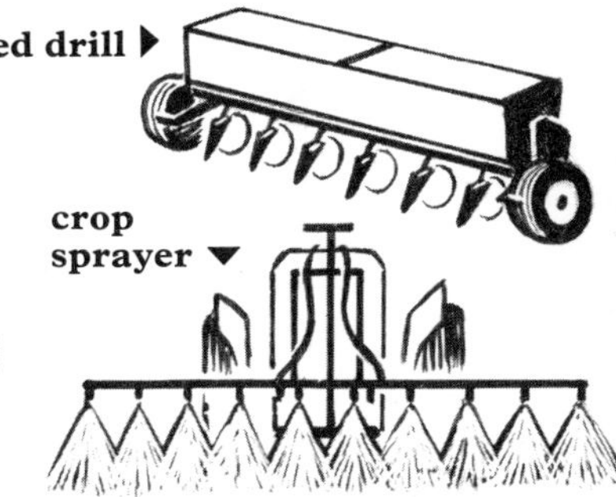

mower

baler

▲ hay turner or "cock pheasant"

elevator

▲

When hay is cut by the **mower,** it is left to dry on the ground. After a day or so it is turned by the **hay turner,** or **cock pheasant** as it is sometimes called. The **baler** compresses the hay into bales and ties them round with string. An **elevator** is often used to ◀ carry the bales to the top of a haystack.

▲

Crop sprays are used to kill weeds and insects. Other implements and machines apply fertilisers, plant potatoes, cut thistles.

The **forage harvester** cuts ▶ green crops for silage, chops them into fine pieces and blows them into a trailer running alongside.

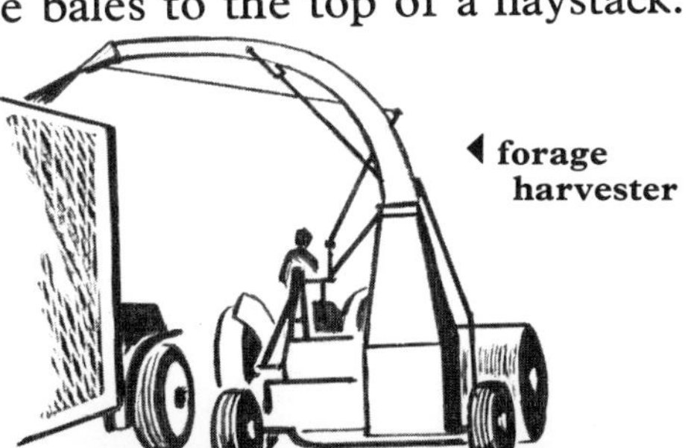

The **combine harvester** cuts the corn and threshes it. ▼

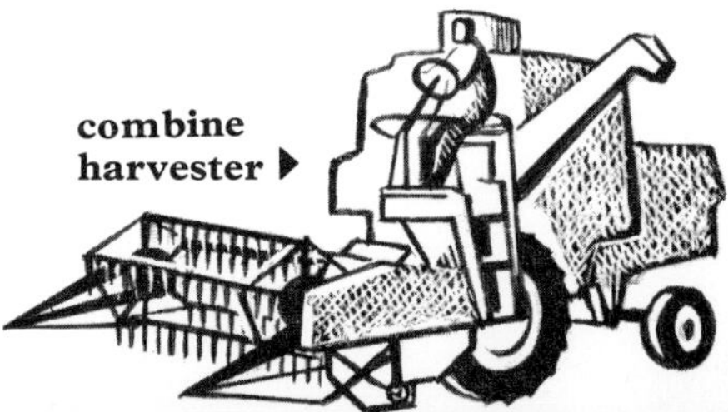

CROPS: CEREALS, ROOTS

The main crops on a farm are illustrated in the pictures on these pages.

Wheat is usually sown in the autumn and harvested in August or September. It thrives in rich soils and in warm dry regions. Farmers prefer to grow it on relatively flat land and in large fields in order to be able to use large modern machines. ▼

Oats can be sown either in the spring or the autumn. They can be grown in relatively poor land and in wetter climates than wheat and barley. They are the most common type of cereal in the hilly lands of the north and west. ▼

Rye is rarely grown in the British Isles. Where it is grown, it is usually on poor land unsuitable for other cereal crops. ▼

wheatfield

wheat barley oats

stooks of oats

rye maize

▲ **Barley** is usually sown in the spring and harvested in August or September. It is used chiefly as fodder for animals, although some is used in making beer. Barley is not quite as demanding as wheat, but the general growing conditions are much the same.

▲ **Maize** is primarily a hot summer cereal and grows best in much warmer climates. However, new varieties are being successfully developed.

CROPS: GRASSES, FRUITS, VEGETABLES

These pictures illustrate some of the principal grasses in the British Isles. Well over one hundred different grasses grow in these islands, but the most important from a farming point of view are the **rye grasses, fescues, cocksfoot** and **timothy grass.**

rye grass

fescue

cocksfoot

timothy grass

FARM BUILDINGS: PAST AND PRESENT

Oast houses can be seen particularly in Kent. They were originally used for drying hops. Many of the buildings have been since converted into houses. ▶

▲ The **tithe barn** is usually close to the village church. It was built to hold the tithe of corn (and other produce)—usually an offering of one-tenth of the harvest given by the peasants to the Church in the Middle Ages.

Sometimes you can see an old **barn** which rests on **staddle stones.** This was to stop rats and other vermin getting at the corn. It also helped to keep the grain dry as air circulated below the granary. ▼

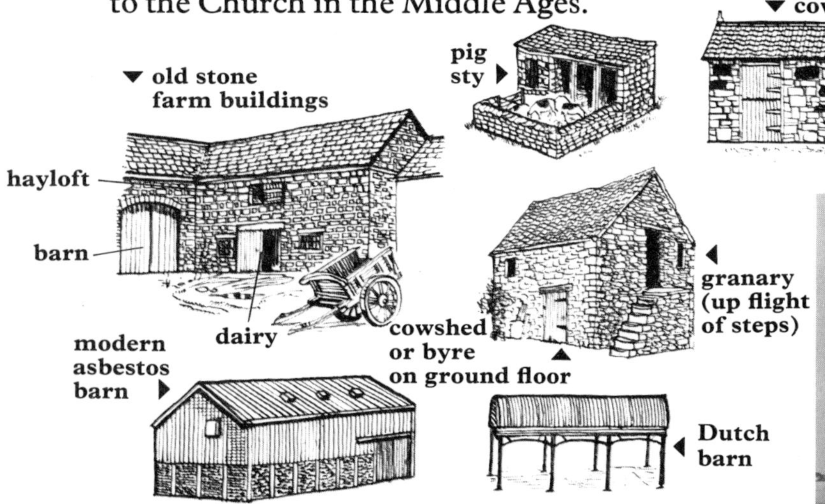

Many other old **barns, cowhouses, Dutch barns, granaries** and **stables** can be seen.

◀ **Silos** are used to store silage—the green crops (usually grass) which are chopped into fragments and kept to provide a rich food for animals in winter.

◀ Methods of storing hay vary from district to district. **Round haystacks** are popular in the West Country; **rectangular stacks** like bread loaves are common in the east. In most parts of the country hay is often stored in modern **concrete buildings.**

▲ **Wind pumps** are used to raise water for use on the farm.

▲ Potatoes and other root crops are often stored in a heap which is triangular in shape if you cut across it. These heaps are long, a metre or so in height, and usually covered with straw to prevent frost getting at them. They are called **clamps,** although in some parts of Britain they are known as **pits** or **pies.**

◀ Modern **dairy parlours** are often highly mechanised—the cows enter under strict control, are milked cleanly and quickly and then leave by a fixed route. The milk is piped direct to the dairy.

◀ **Cattle grids** are constructed so that vehicles can pass over them but not the hooves of cattle or other animals.

CATTLE BREEDS

Cattle can be divided into three main types.

Dairy breeds are noted either for their heavy yields of milk or for the richness of their milk. Dairy cattle usually have longer legs than beef cattle and they appear to be broader at the rear.

Beef breeds are noted either for their ability to turn fodder into meat quickly or for the quality of their meat. They generally appear to have shorter legs than the dairy breeds and have rather square, fat bodies.

Dual-purpose breeds are cattle whose milking qualities are good and yet they still produce an acceptable carcase for the butcher. Some dairy breeds produce meat which is almost impossible to sell in a butcher's shop, while some beef breeds have cows whose milk yields and milk quality are not a paying proposition for a dairy farmer. Dual-purpose breeds are therefore useful animals to rear, but frequently a farmer crosses his breeds to get the best possible result for his own situation. Thus a dairy farmer may keep a dairy herd of excellent milkers, but by crossing them with a beef bull can sell or rear the calves for butcher's meat.

PIGS, HORSES, POULTRY, SHEEP

Work horses are not often found on modern farms, although they have advantages compared with the tractor particularly on very heavy land or on steep slopes. Horses for **riding, hunting** and **racing** are usually more common.

The main breeds of pigs are illustrated in these pictures. **Porker pigs** are killed at about 80kg, **bacon pigs** at about 110kg, and **sausage pigs** at anything from 125kg upwards.

These are the chief sheep breeds of the British Isles. Some are noted for the quantity or quality of their wool, others are noted for their meat, some are noted for their ability to breed, and some are kept for their ability to survive almost any type of winter weather out of doors.

These are some of the principal breeds of **ducks** and **chickens,** although nowadays chickens are rarely seen in large numbers outside the **broiler house** or **battery** or **deep litter unit.**

STILES AND GATES

It is remarkable just how many different types of stile and gate can be found within a relatively small area. The pictures show just a few of the many varieties to be discovered.

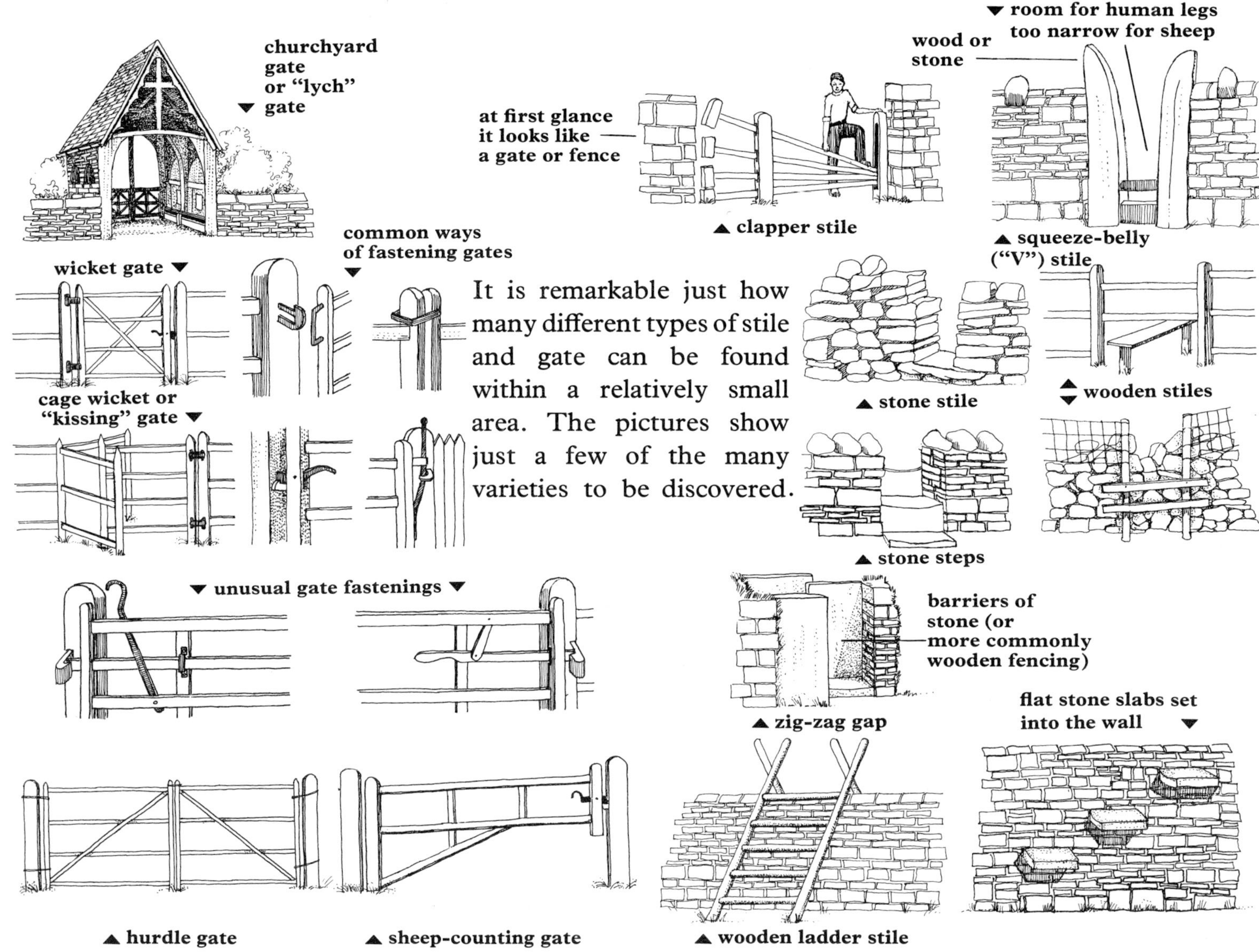

FIELD BOUNDARIES

Many **walls** and **hedges** were erected after the open fields were enclosed. Most date back to the great period of enclosure from about 1750 to 1830. **Dry stone** walls with large uneven boulders at their base and assorted stones above are usually much older than dry stone walls composed of stones of roughly equal shape and size. Sometimes you can see loose stones blocking up a V-shaped opening in the wall. This is a **cow creep**. Holes at the base of dry stone walls are known as **hogg holes** and young sheep can use them to go from one field to another.

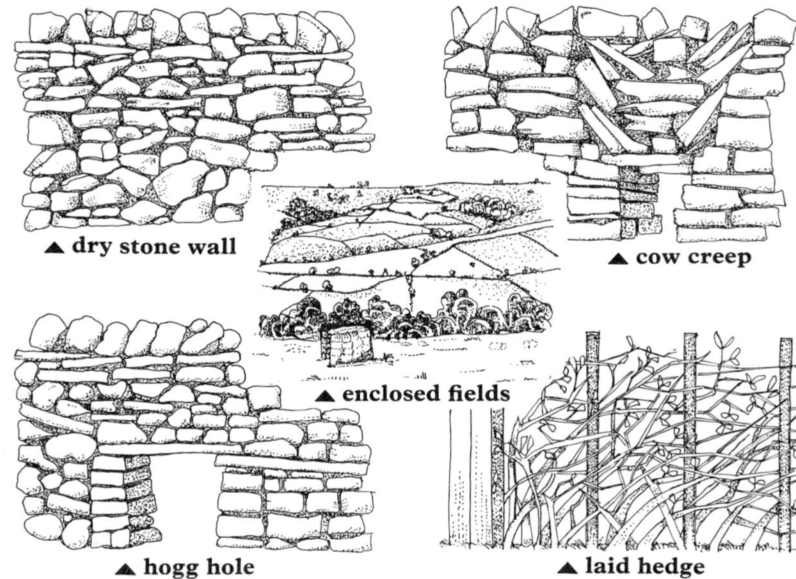

▲ dry stone wall

▲ cow creep

▲ enclosed fields

▲ hogg hole

▲ laid hedge

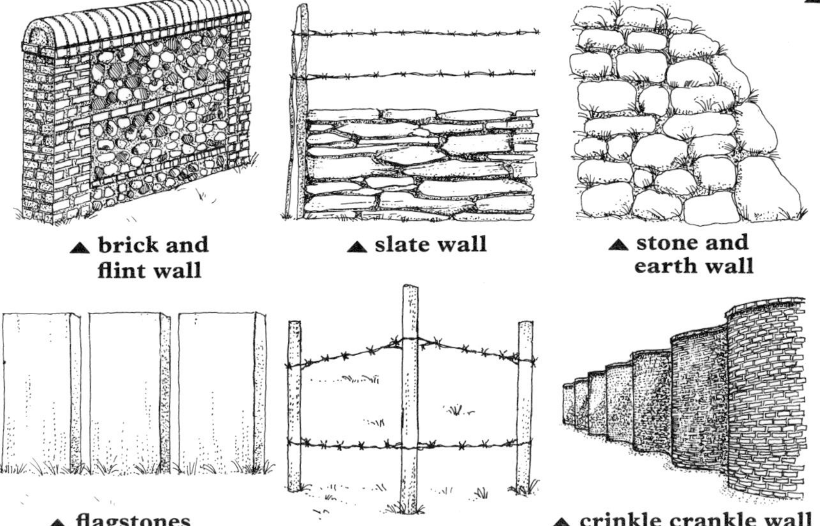

▲ brick and flint wall

▲ slate wall

▲ stone and earth wall

▲ flagstones

▲ barbed wire

▲ crinkle crankle wall

Hedges are laid by planting small hedge shrubs in a course which is supported by branches laid on the ground. Very old hedges often have several different types of shrub growing there within a relatively short distance.

Other types of field boundary include walls made of **brick and flint, slate walls, earth and stone walls** or **dykes,** walls made up of **flagstones,** and, of course, barbed wire fences. In some places it is possible to see walls which resemble a switchback. These are called **crinkle crankle walls.**

PREHISTORIC BURIAL GROUNDS

Prehistoric burial places can be found in many parts of the British Isles. Sometimes the burial places were composed of large blocks of stone which formed chambers such as those shown in the pictures below. There are several different types of **meg-lithic burial chamber** as they are called. Some are huge cairns of stones, others have just a small group of stones standing. Where there is just a solitary chamber left, it is called a **dolmen** (Scotland and Ireland) or **cromlech** (Wales). The burial grounds were usually covered with huge piles of earth. In many cases the earth has been moved and the stones are all that remains. There are two main types of **burial mound.** The **long barrows** are up to 100 metres long and 30 metres wide. They are less common than the **round barrows** which are smaller and range in size from about 5 metres to 30 metres in length. There are various types of round barrow such as the bell barrows (for men), disc barrows (for women) and bowl barrows. Barrows are often shown on Ordnance Survey maps as **tumuli.** They are often difficult to identify as such in the field for they can be easily confused with **drumlins** which have a similar shape (see page 103).

megalithic tomb ▶

long barrow ▼

▼ round barrows ▼

▲ 1. bowl

▲ 2. bell

▲ 3. disc

▲ dolmen or cromlech

▼ tumulus

PREHISTORIC FORTS, STRONGHOLDS, VILLAGES

▲ Iron Age fort (Maiden Castle)

Only sporadic remains of prehistoric settlement can be seen today. They include **iron age villages** such as the settlement at Chysauster in Cornwall, the **prehistoric settlement** at Jarlshof in the Shetlands, or evidence of prehistoric industry as at the prehistoric **flint mines** at Grimes Graves in Norfolk. In Scotland tall round towers called **brochs** can be seen which were used as fortifications in the Iron Age.

The major defensive earthworks of the prehistoric period are to be seen at the great **Iron Age forts**—notably those of southern England, such as at Maiden Castle in Dorset. This was a series of concentric **ditches** and **earth walls** which would originally have been surmounted by wooden **fences. Hill forts** are relatively common but on a much smaller scale than this.

Iron Age village ▼

Grimes Graves flint mines ▼

Scottish broch

STONE CIRCLES AND STANDING STONES

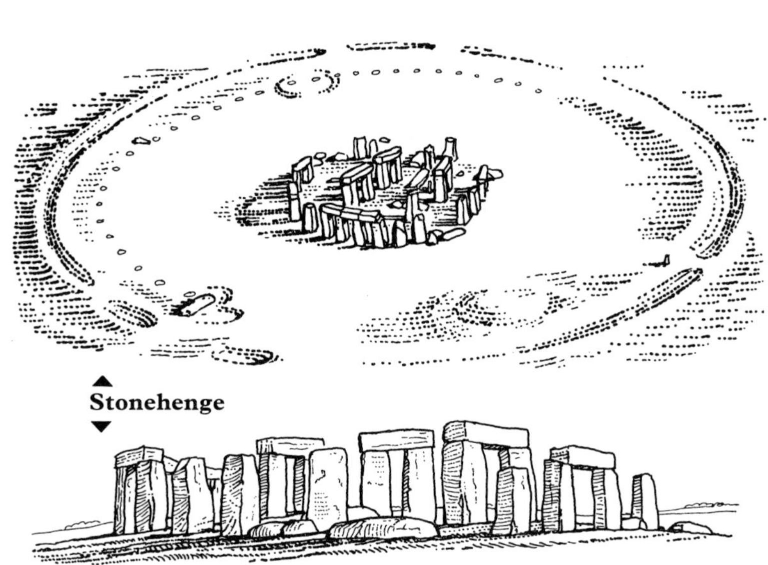

▲ Stonehenge ▼

Some of the most fascinating prehistoric relics are probably the stone circles and avenues of **standing stones** erected by prehistoric men on a wide variety of sites in the British Isles. These are now believed to have been situated with particular regard to the movement of the sun, moon and stars, and probably had some religious significance.

At Stonehenge the direction of the shadows at sunrise on Midsummer Day suggests that the prehistoric men who built the monument were aware of this and designed the layout of the stones accordingly. **Henges** (such as Stonehenge) differ from ordinary stone circles in that they have a **ditch** surrounding them. Standing stones (often known as **monoliths** or **menhirs**) often occur in **rows** and **avenues.** Where they stand on their own, it is assumed they had some religious significance or that they may even have been statues or memorials to a chieftain.

▲ stone circle

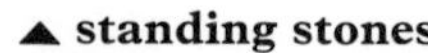

▲ standing stones

▲ avenue of standing stones

▲ stone row

FIELD PATTERNS AND MARKINGS

▲ Celtic fields

▲ lynchets

ridge and furrow ▼

In the fields you can sometimes see **ridges, terraces** and **undulations.** You may rightly suspect that they are not natural and that they were formed many centuries ago. However, it is not easy to say when precisely they were formed or why.

The so-called **Celtic fields** are relics of the Iron Age and the Roman period. These were relatively small, squarish fields and they show up best in aerial photographs. On the ground they are not at all easy to identify.

Lynchets are terraces which may be of medieval date or even earlier. They may have been formed when primitive ploughing loosened the soil, and soil creep caused the soil to move down the slope to form a sequence of terraces. On the other hand the slopes may have been terraced to be easier to farm.

In many pasturelands, particularly on clay, you can see parallel **ridges and furrows.** These are relics of the days when the fields were ploughed as part of the open field system.

On some stones in the north you can sometimes see the peculiar **"cup and ring"** markings.

In chalk country prehistoric man discovered that by cutting away the vegetation and top soil lying on the surface he could expose the white chalk below and create giant figures such as the **white horses** and **long men** of the southern downlands.

▲ cup and ring markings

▲ figures carved
▼ in chalk hillside

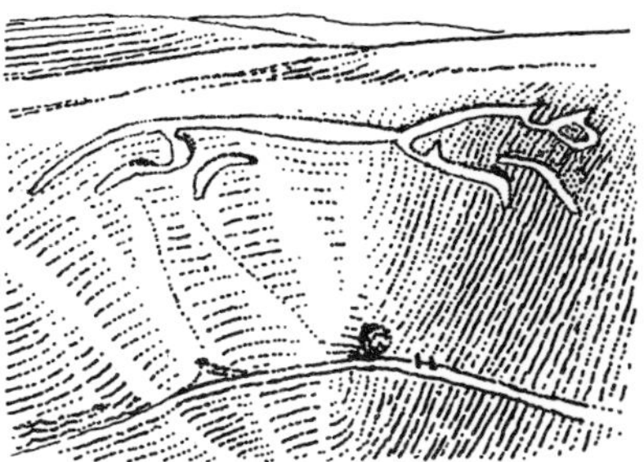

ROMAN REMAINS

Roman armies were highly organised. When they rested for the night they erected a **temporary camp** on similar lines to their permanent **forts.** These always followed the same basic plan. In the centre they erected the **headquarters building** and close by the **villa** for the fort commander. On the other side they built the central **storehouses** and **granaries.** Sometimes **workshops,** the **bathhouse** and a **hospital** were situated in this area. **Barracks** and **stables** formed the other buildings which lay within a rectangular site surrounded by a wall or fence. Straight roads made a geometrical pattern as they criss-crossed the camp.

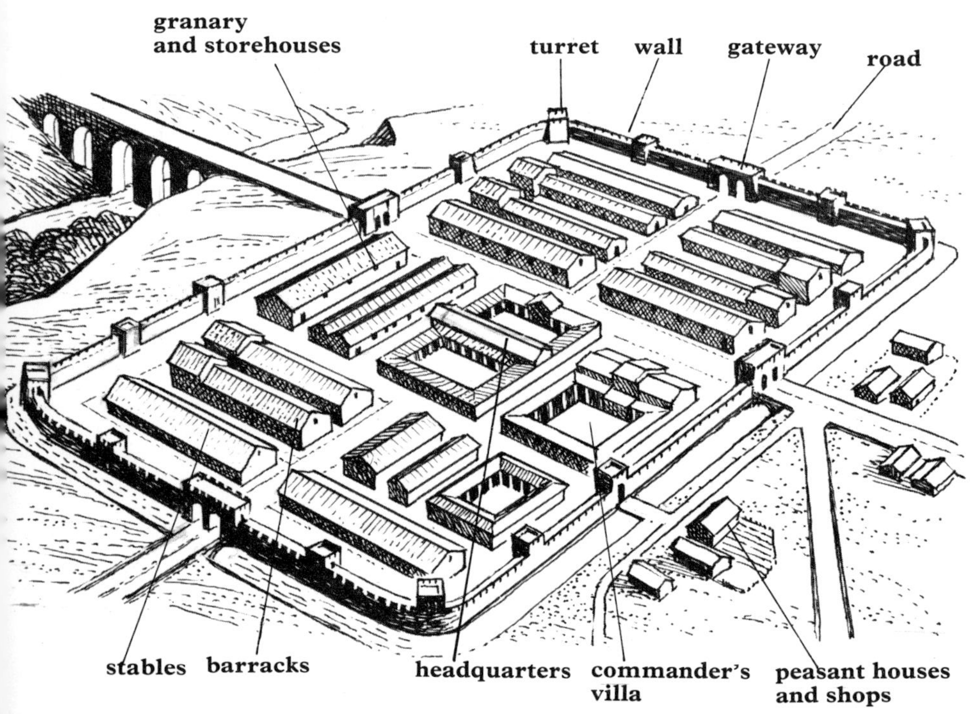

A ROMAN FORT

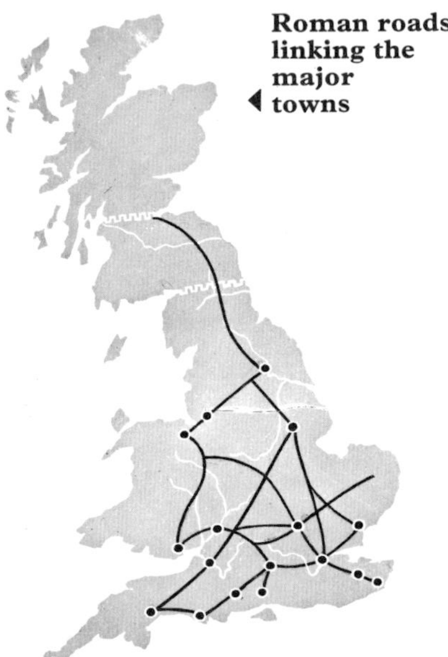

Roman roads linking the major towns

Roman **roads** tended to be straight and in hilly country this meant that they frequently took a very undulating course. Many modern roads follow the same line across country.

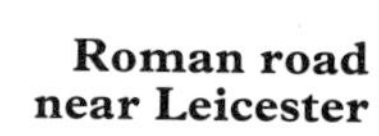

Roman road near Leicester

▲ Many modern cities were founded in Roman times. Roman towns always had a central area or **forum** with shops, courts and a hall.

Roman **baths** and **bath-houses** were forerunners of Turkish and sauna baths. A well preserved bath-house can be seen at Chesters in Northumberland, and famous baths at Bath, Somerset. ▲

Roman **amphitheatres** can be seen at St. Albans and Caerleon.

Hadrian's Wall was built from Tyneside to the Solway Firth in order to protect the land to the south from the warlike Picts who lived to the north. ▲

The remains of Roman **villas** are often difficult to picture. There is a well known villa at Lullingstone in Kent, with many **mosaics.** ▼

The later Romans were Christians but remains of the earlier **pagan temples** can sometimes be seen such as the temple to Mithras at Carrawburgh on Hadrian's Wall. ▼

SURNAMES

The surnames that can be seen on the **shop fronts** of a town or in a town's **telephone directory** are often worth looking at a little more closely. Surnames generally fall into four main categories:

(*a*) those derived from the **first name** of the **father** such as Richardson (Richard's son) or just Richards (Richard's) or even Dickson (Dick's son) or Dicks (Dick's). These are called **patronyms,**

(*b*) those named after **trades, industries** and other forms of **employment** such as . . .
the woollen industry: Walker, Weaver, Fuller, Webb, Webster;
craftsmen: Wright, Smith, Cartwright, Wheelwright, Thatcher, Mason;
shopkeepers: Baker, Merchant, Butcher;
servants and officials: Clark, Chamberlain, Steward, Squires,

(*c*) those named after **place-names** such as London and Kent or after **natural features** such as Wood, Tree and Lake or after **man-made features** such as Castle, Church, Wall and Street,

(*d*) those names which owe their origin to **personal characteristics** such as Longfellow, Short, Brown, Redhead and Strong.

PLACENAMES

Most of the towns and villages in the British Isles were named before the Norman Conquest in 1066. Only a few towns have names which owe their origin to the **French** language of the Normans (for example, Belvoir). A few towns have **Roman** names (for example, Doncaster and other places ending in -caster and -chester). Most towns have either **Anglo Saxon** names or **Danish** names. You can tell this from the endings of place names.

The first Anglo Saxon villages were founded near the south-east coast of England and up river valleys. These villages and towns have names ending in **ing** as in Dorking, Hastings, Lancing and Worthing. Villages founded slightly later than this often have names ending in **ham** (as in Chatham) or in **ton** (as in Kingston). Some places have names which are a combination of these endings such as Dersingham, Northampton, Workington.

Some village names have endings which meant meadow or clearing in a forest such as **ley** as in Shipley or in **field** as in Sheffield. Other placenames have endings which mean island (**ney** as in Walney) or hill (**don** as in Swindon) or ford(**ford** as in Brentford).

Danish placenames usually end in either **by** (as in Derby and Corby) or in **thorpe** (as in Scunthorpe and Cleethorpes).

CRAFTS

In these pictures you can see some of the old crafts which you would have seen in most towns and villages a hundred years or so ago. Sometimes it is possible to see signs of these crafts today.

▲ The **basketmaker** used reeds and osiers to make many different types of container and items of furniture.

▲ The **blacksmith** worked with metals. His main job was often that of shoeing horses (strictly the job of a **farrier**). In rural areas today a blacksmith will find plenty of work.

▲ **Thatchers** are still in great demand for their services. There are still thousands of thatched cottages left in Britain.

The **cooper** made wooden barrels. ▼

◀ The **wheelwright** made and repaired cart wheels.

CUSTOMS

The customs you can see celebrated today in different parts of the country often date back hundreds of years. Many of these customs derive from **superstitions** or to **fears** that a source of supply may dry up (such as the Derbyshire well dressing customs). Some customs are **religious** in character such as the Harvest Festival, although even these are sometimes **pagan** in origin.

Dancing round the maypole on May Day is a custom going right back to pagan times. ▲

Morris dancing. ▲

The Bacup coconut dancers dance every Eastertime.

The Derbyshire well dressing ceremonies date back to the time when the survival of a village depended on its water supply. ▼

The Ambleside rush-bearing ceremony in July celebrates an old custom when rushes covered the church floor.

In September the Abbots Bromley horn dancers dance with reindeer horns on their heads. ▼

◀ At Padstow May Day is celebrated by the Hobby Horse festival.

Every Shrove Tuesday a pancake race is held at Olney.

On New Year's Eve the men of Allendale in Northumberland celebrate the end of the old year by walking in procession with blazing tubs of tar on their heads.

HERALDRY

Coats of arms follow the same basic plan illustrated in the diagram below. This is called a full **achievement of arms** and comprises a central **shield** supported by two beasts (or **supporters**) standing above a **motto.** On top of the shield there is first of all a **helm,** then a **mantling** and finally a **crest.** On either side there may be **badges.** The heraldic **devices** and the **emblems** used often have a particular significance for the family or organisation concerned.

crest

helm

supporter

mantling

POWER IN TRUST

motto

shield or coat of arms

▲ barry  ▲ paly  ▲ bendy  ▲ gyronny  ▲ checky

▲ per fesse  ▲ per pale  ▲ per bend  ▲ per Chevron  ▲ per saltire  ▲ per cross or quarterly

The shields have various **patterns** as you can see in the small pictures.

▲ lion rampant

▲ lion passant

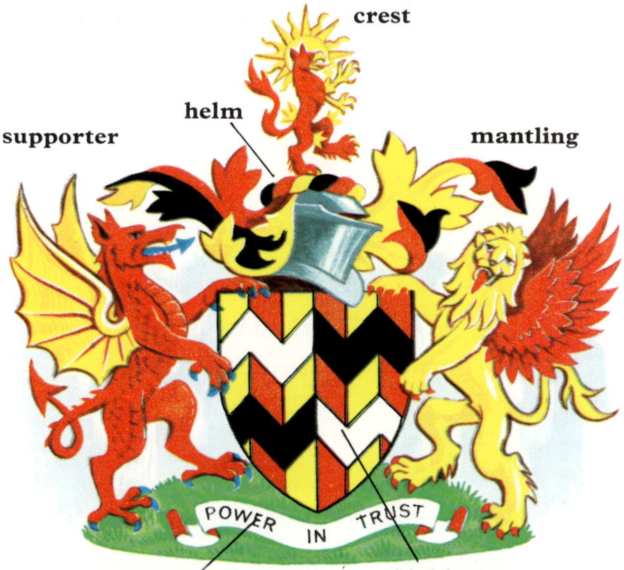

▲ lion couchant

▲ cross fleury ▲ cross crosslet

▲ cinq foil (5 leaves)  ▲ fleur-de-lis

▲ badge of the Order of St. John of Jerusalem (Maltese cross)

THE WEATHER

CLOUDS

Clouds often give a clue to the weather we are likely to get. **Cirrus** clouds often foreshadow the passing of a depression or changeable weather. This is heralded by the arrival of **altocumulus, altostratus,** and **stratus,** the sheet clouds. Rain is usually imminent when the rain clouds **nimbostratus** and **cumulonimbus** can be seen. **Cumulus** clouds are generally fair weather clouds.

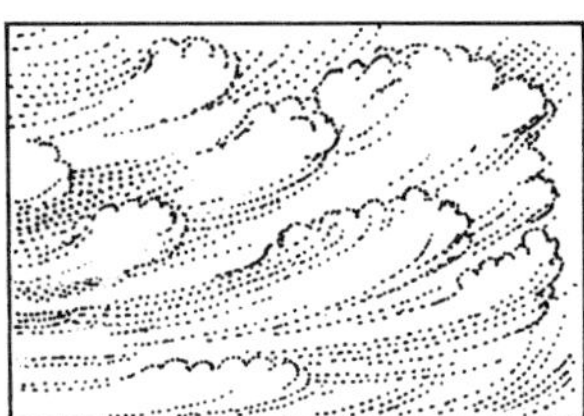

▲ cirrus

▲ cumulus

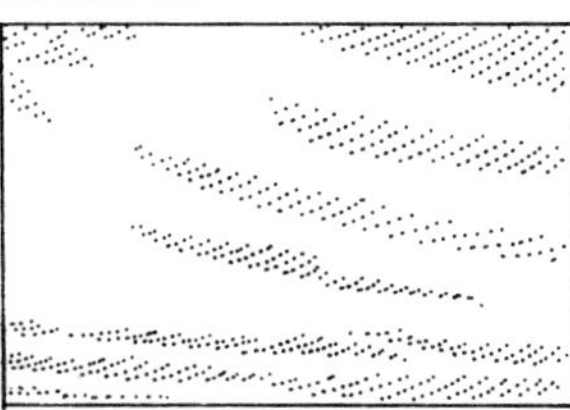

▲ stratus

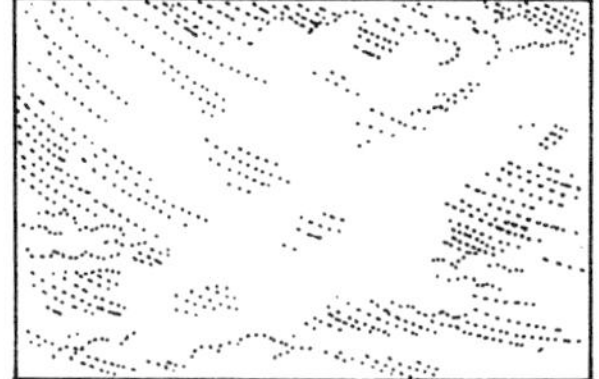

▲ cirro-stratus

▲ nimbo-stratus

▲ cumulo-nimbus

WIND

Wind force can be estimated by using this table.

FORCE ▼	DESCRIPTION ▼	EFFECTS ▼
0	**Calm:**	Smoke rises vertically
1	**Light Air:**	Smoke shows wind direction
2	**Light Breeze:**	Wind felt on face.
3	**Gentle Breeze:**	Leaves moving.
4	**Moderate Breeze:**	Litter moved.
5	**Fresh Breeze:**	Small trees sway.
6	**Strong Breeze:**	Large branches sway.
7	**Near Gale:**	Difficult to walk against.
8	**Gale:**	Twigs break off trees.
9	**Strong Gale:**	Slates blown off.
10	**Whole Gale:**	Trees uprooted—rare.

VISIBILITY

The extent of visibility can easily be judged from this table provided certain marker points are noted in advance when the visibility is excellent (e.g. 200 metres to the Church).

DISTANCE YOU CAN SEE ▼	TYPE ▼
less than 40 m	**Dense Fog**
40–200 m	**Thick Fog**
200–1000 m	**Fog**
1–2 km	**Mist**
2–4 km	**Poor Visibility**
4–10 km	**Moderate Visibility**
more than 10 km	**Good Visibility**

HILLS, Valleys, ROUTEWAYS

PANORAMA: HILLS AND VALLEYS

corrie
hanging valley
scree
U-shaped valley
terracettes
source of stream
spur
waterfall
drumlins
tributary stream
finger lake
confluence
terraces
terminal moraine
bridge
meander
peat cuttings
bridge
road
lacustrine delta

plateau
back slope
(or dip slope)
escarpment
(scarp)
reservoir
hydro-
electric
power
station
dam
forest
cairn
lake
heather

THE SUMMIT OF A HILL

The pictures on these pages show some of the features to be seen when walking in hill country.

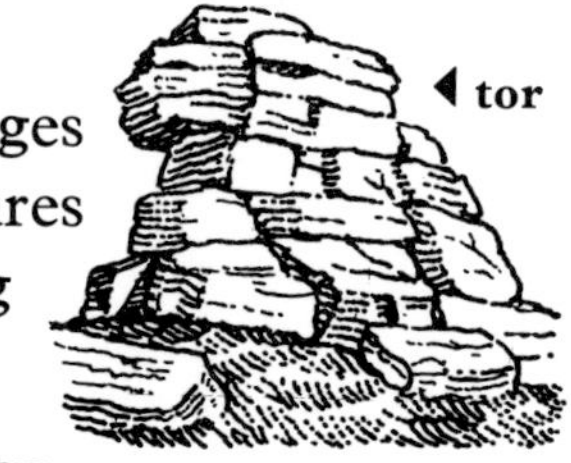

scarp
dip slope
plateau
spur
ridge
saddle
col
knoll
gorge

V-shaped valley

convex slope
concave slope

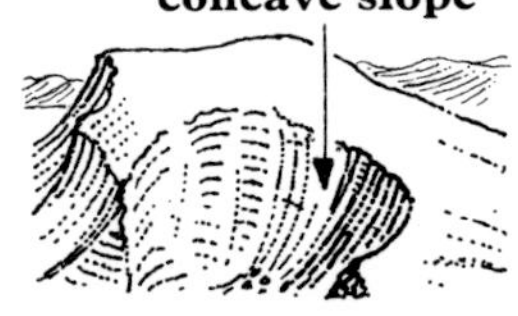

In Cornwall you can sometimes see weathered rock caps on the summits of hills. These are **tors** and they are formed on granite moorlands. They are not to be confused with the **cairns of stones** which mark the summits of hills in many mountain areas.

triangulation point

·275 spot height

bench mark

On an Ordnance Survey map you will often see hill summits marked by a triangle, dot and height. This is a **triangulation point.** Other heights are shown by **spot heights** and **bench marks.**

POINTS TO REMEMBER WHEN WALKING IN THE HILLS

1. **Let someone know where you are going and when you expect to be back.**
2. **Take a companion with you.**
3. **Take Ordnance Survey maps, a compass, a whistle, warm clothing, waterproofs, boots, an emergency supply of food (such as chocolate).**
4. **Know the mountain code of safety; take heed of the weather forecast for the area; don't climb if you can't read a map or use a compass.**
5. **Don't ignore these simple precautions. It may be hot, clear and sunny first thing in the morning at ground level. It may be cold and misty when you reach the summit.**

MOUNTAIN VEGETATION

These are pictures of some of the common types of hill or mountain vegetation to be seen in the British Isles.

peat bog

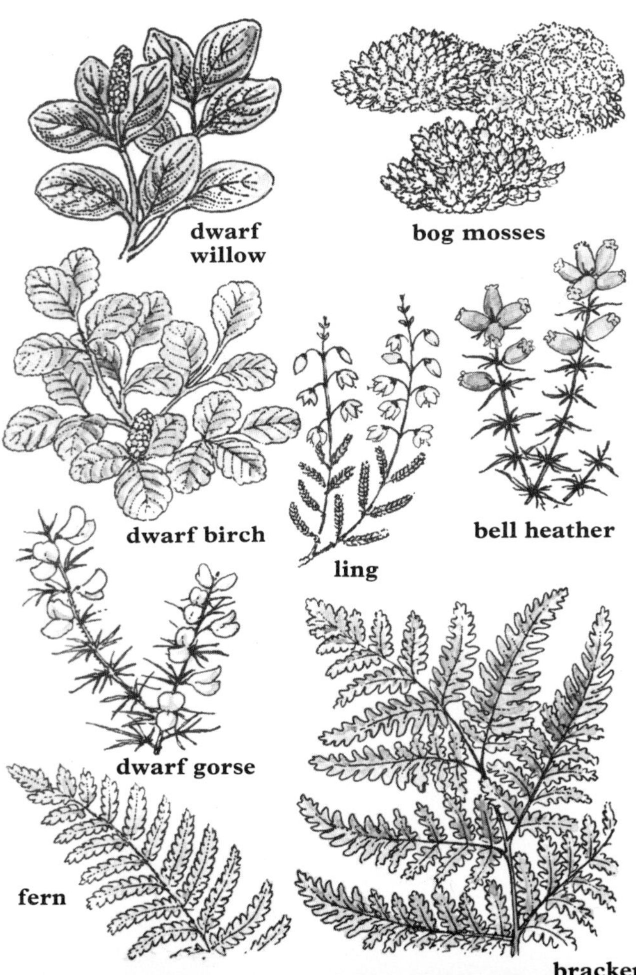

WEATHERING

The effects of the weather on rocks can be seen when walking in the hills. When water freezes at night in the cracks and crevices in the rock face, it expands and breaks off tiny pieces of rock. This frost-shattered rock tumbles down the slope to form piles of rock known as **scree.**

▲ scree

▲ frost-shattering

▲ exposed tree roots

terracettes ▼

Sometimes **tree roots** are exposed when soil is washed away by rain water or removed by the action of the wind.

When the soil is very wet, it may slide slowly and imperceptibily downhill. It may take many years before these **terracettes** (see picture) are formed. They are sometimes wrongly described as being **sheep tracks.**

SOIL

Soil is formed from rock. If you look at a layer of soil which has been exposed, you can often see the **bedrock** at the bottom and then layers of **sub-soil** and **top soil.**

darker soil, fertile, rich in humus (decaying plants), softer to the touch, worms and insects live here	**top soil**
weathered soil, usually lighter in colour, harder in texture, often contains hard pan (soil layer cemented together)	**sub-soil**
often broken and weathered rock at first merging with solid bedrock below	**bedrock**

SCENERY DUE TO ROCKS

These pictures show typical landscapes which arise from the characteristics of certain types of rock. Rocks which allow water to soak through or to escape through cracks are called **permeable** and they usually lack running water and ponds on the surface. Because there is a dearth of surface water they often lack trees. **Chalk** and **limestone** are the principal permeable rocks although some areas have **loose sands** as their surface rock and these soak up water rapidly. Rocks such as **clay** are highly impermeable and because of this they feature **trees,** lush **grassland, ditches** and **ponds.**

The **harder** the rock, the more likely it is that the landscape will be **hilly.** Relatively soft sandstones give rise to rolling country, very hard sandstones produce rugged scenery. Volcanic rocks are generally the toughest rocks and they provide varied rugged mountain landscapes, although even here there are differences between the types of rock. In the island of Skye the granite mountains are rounder than the sharp serrated Cuillins which are formed from tougher gabbro.

▼ **volcanic rocks in North Wales**

▼ **granite in Northern Scotland**

◀ carboniferous limestone in the Pennines—limestone exposed on the surface (scars), dry valleys (most of the streams flow underground), potholes and underground caverns

sandstone—undulating ▶

◀ oolitic limestone in the Cotswolds (steep escarpments, dry valleys and gentle dip slopes)

soft sands—pine trees ▶

◀ chalk downland in Sussex, dry valleys (valleys without streams), chalk quarries, cement works, rolling hills and rounded slopes

clay farm land—ponds, trees, shallow slopes ▶

A glaciated valley

Ice covered most of the British Isles over 10,000 years ago. Glaciers carved **valleys** and left their mark on the landscape, particularly in the mountain areas of Wales, the Lake District and Scotland. Some of these effects can be seen in the pictures on these pages, and on pages 96-97.

▲

Corrie and **arête.** A **corrie** is a deep hollow high up in the hills which was etched deep by the work of ice. Ice collected here and fed the glacier in the valley below. As the ice moved downhill, it pulled away at the sides of the corrie and rock was also loosened by water freezing in the rock joints and cracks. The wall of rock between two adjacent corries got progressively sharper and this sharp-edged ridge is known today as an **arête.**

▲

Hanging valley. Tributary **streams** often plunge through **waterfalls** and **rapids** to the lake or river on the floor of the glaciated valley.

▲

U-shaped valley and **finger lake.** The valleys carved and deepened by glaciers are usually **U-shaped.** They often contain a long narrow lake known as a **finger lake** or **ribbon lake.** ▶

▲

Roche moutonnée. When ice slid over a knob of rock on the ground, it scratched and scraped the near side smooth but plucked away at the other side (the short, stub end).

▲

Striations. The glacier carried large boulders and these pressed down on to small sharp stones which scratched long lines called **striations** on the smooth rock below the glacier.

Erratics. When scree stones and boulders fell on the glacier they were carried forward. When the ice melted, these stones lay in new positions many kilometres away from their point of origin. ▼

Boulder clay. The material scraped and carried by a glacier is often a yellowish/brownish mixture of stones and soil known as **boulder clay.** ▼

▲

Terminal moraines. When the glacier carried forward large deposits of boulder clay, these were dumped at the point where the ice melted to form long ridges across the valley.

▲

Drumlins. These are low rounded mounds of boulder clay which usually occur in groups and resemble eggs from the air. They were probably formed by glaciers riding over earlier terminal moraines and shaping them.

On the valley floor

bog bean

The floor of a valley is usually **flat.** In its natural state it is **damp** and **waterlogged. Grass** grows well and also water-loving plants such as those to be seen in marshland areas **:reeds, sedges, rushes** and **willow trees.**

Usually the valley floor has been drained by **dykes** and **ditches** and these are shown on Ordnance Survey maps by small straight blue lines.

broadleaved pond weed

horsetail

flowering rush

soft rush

marsh orchid

water forget-me-not

Land reclamation

In the extensive areas of lowlying land such as the Fenland regions of Norfolk, Cambridgeshire and Lincolnshire you can see the intensive efforts which have been made to drain and reclaim the fen. Much new rich **farmland** has been created from areas which were formerly damp peat areas or flooded marshlands. Long **dykes** were cut to drain the land; **pumping stations** (formerly windmills) pumped the water from the dykes into the rivers which emptied into the sea. The rivers have usually been **straightened** in order to deepen their course and to eliminate the possibilities of floods. Sometimes **sluice gates** control the flow, allowing water to escape from the dykes at low tide into the rivers but not allowing tidal water to enter the dykes at high tide.

▼ **dyke or drain**

▼ **pumping station**

▼ **sluice gates**

A reservoir

Some reservoirs are formed by raising the level of existing lakes.

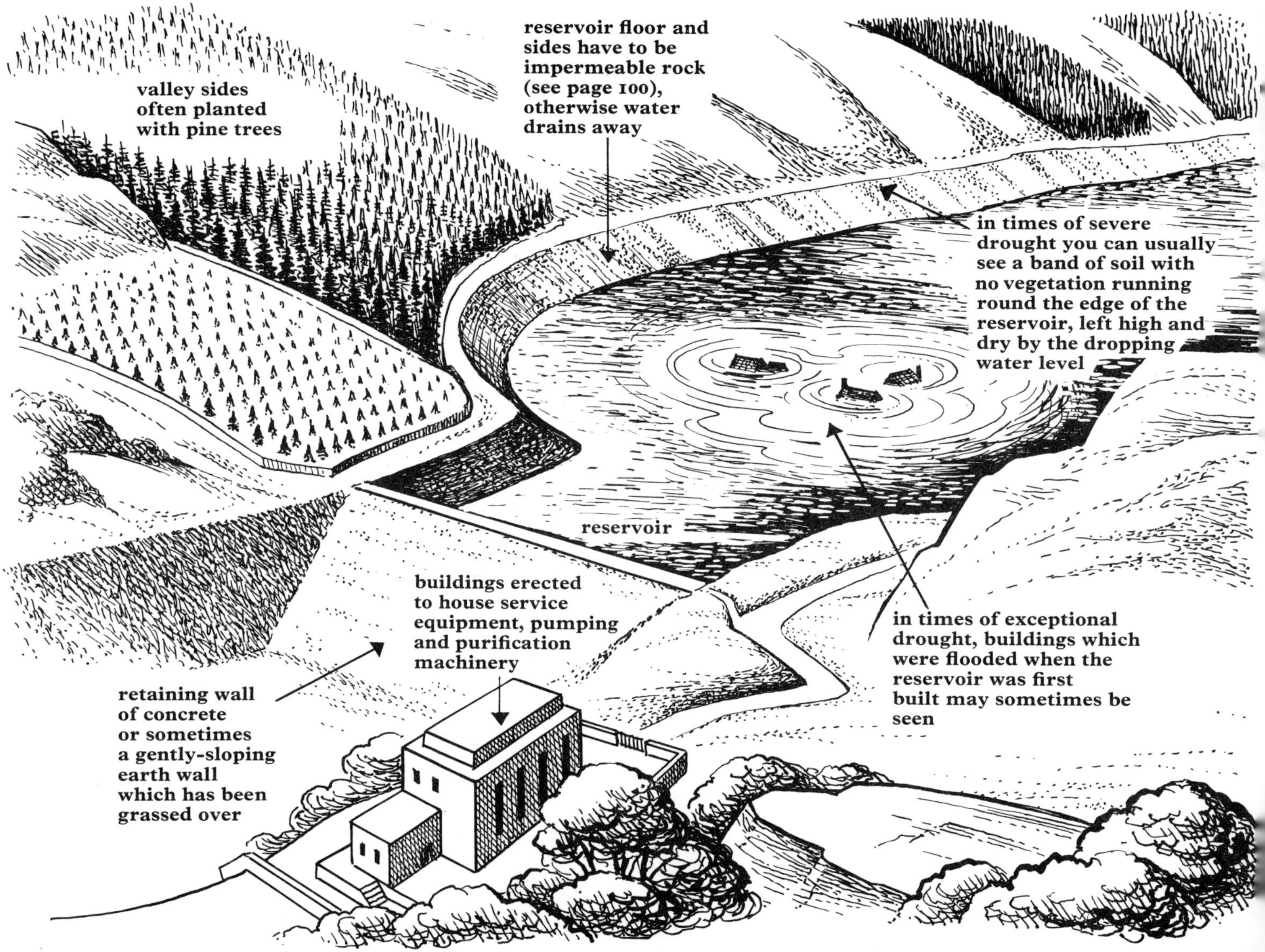

valley sides often planted with pine trees

reservoir floor and sides have to be impermeable rock (see page 100), otherwise water drains away

in times of severe drought you can usually see a band of soil with no vegetation running round the edge of the reservoir, left high and dry by the dropping water level

reservoir

buildings erected to house service equipment, pumping and purification machinery

in times of exceptional drought, buildings which were flooded when the reservoir was first built may sometimes be seen

retaining wall of concrete or sometimes a gently-sloping earth wall which has been grassed over

Hydro electricity

▲ dam and power station

▲ pipes

Most of the hydro electricity schemes in Britain are situated in the highlands of Scotland. Running water is used to turn the turbines which revolve at high speed to produce electricity. The water is usually taken from a **dam** and passed down thick **pipes** into the **power station.** You can often see these pipes near a hydro electric power station. One of the problems encountered when damming up highland rivers is that such a scheme interferes with the natural life of the stream. **Salmon ladders** are sometimes constructed to allow the salmon to swim up an artificial river at the side of the dam. The salmon ladder is designed so that it resembles a set of rapids.

diagram of salmon ladder ▼

arrows show direction of flow of current

▼ salmon ladder

A lake

Most lakes in the British Isles have been formed in some way or other as a result of the after effects of the work of ice. Glaciers deepen their valleys and when the ice melts a lake may be created when streams fill the deep hollow. Sometimes terminal moraines block the exit of the river (see page 103) and create a lake. Small lakes (or **tarns**) are often found in corries.

▲ glacial lake

▼ tarn

Freshwater life: in a river

brown trout

crayfish
cotton grass

dipper

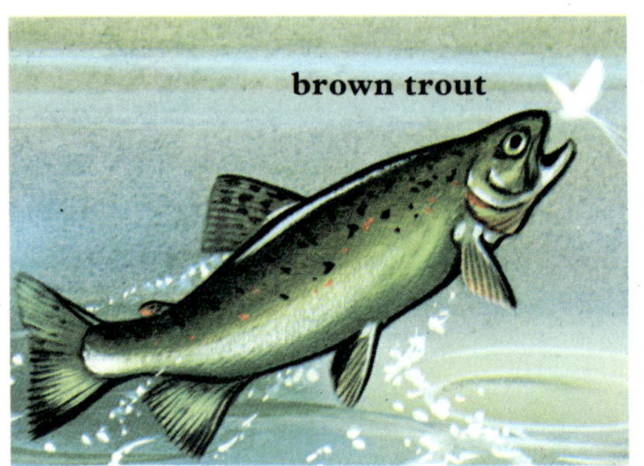

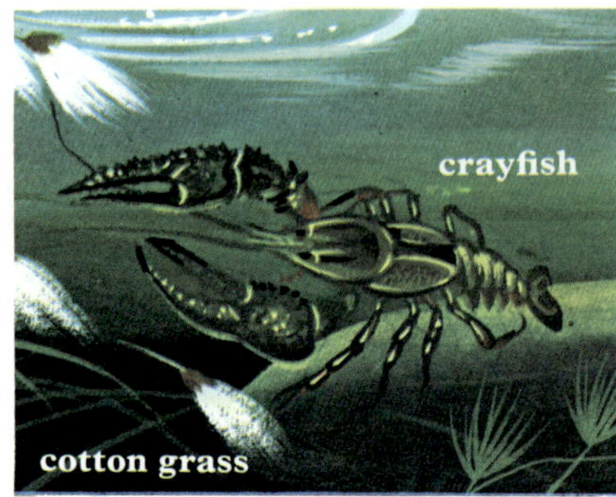

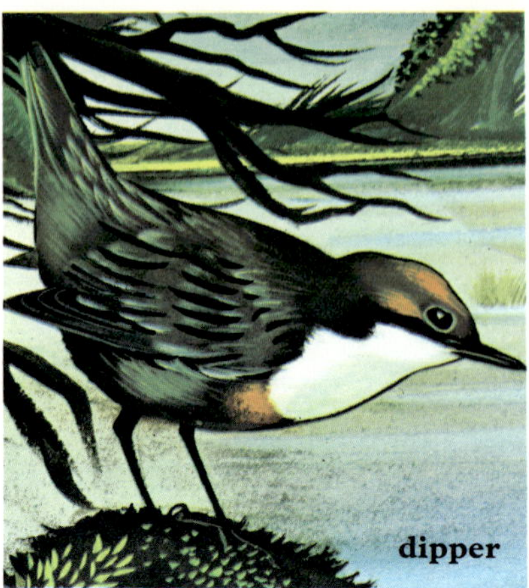

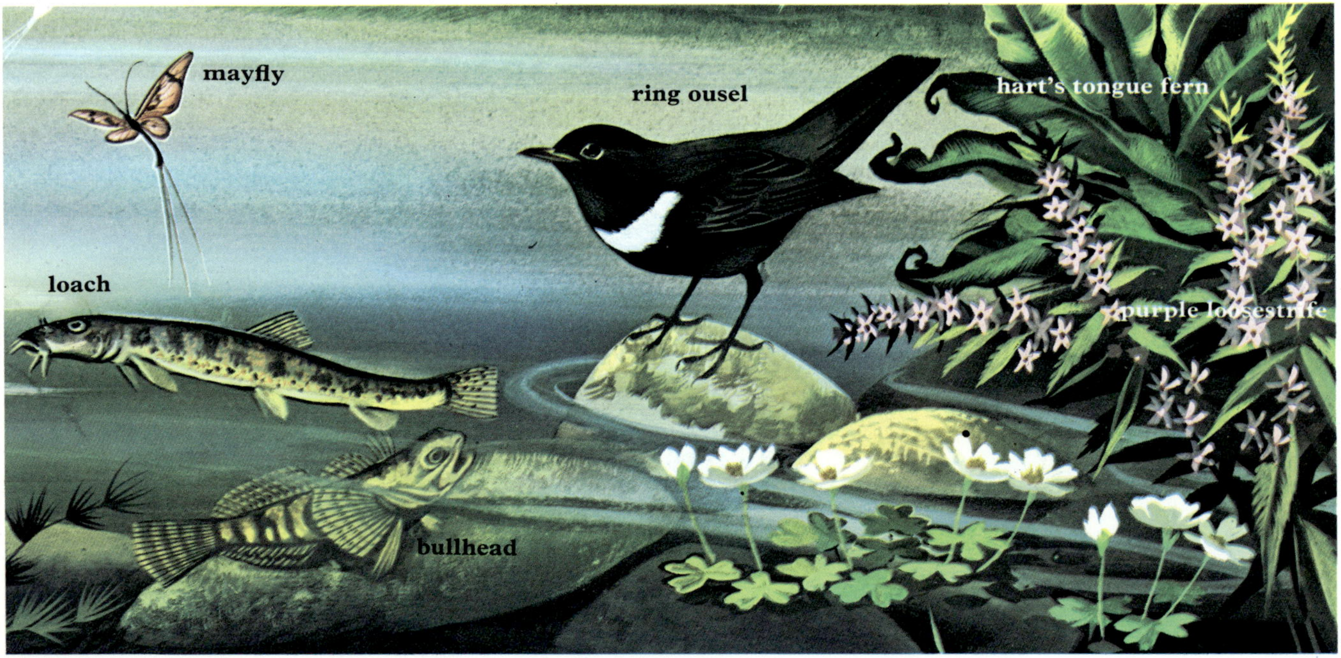

mayfly
ring ousel
hart's tongue fern
loach
purple loosestrife
bullhead

in a pond

frogbit

fringed water lily

great diving beetle

water crowfoot

Canadian pond weed

tadpoles

pond snail

pond snail

dragonfly larva

pond mussel

ramshorn snails

water iris

reed mace

arrowhead

marsh marigold

Rivers

The features to be seen along the course of a river have been given names as you can see in the diagrams on these pages.

Waterfalls

deep plunge pool
undercutting
pebbles deposited in shallower, slower section downstream

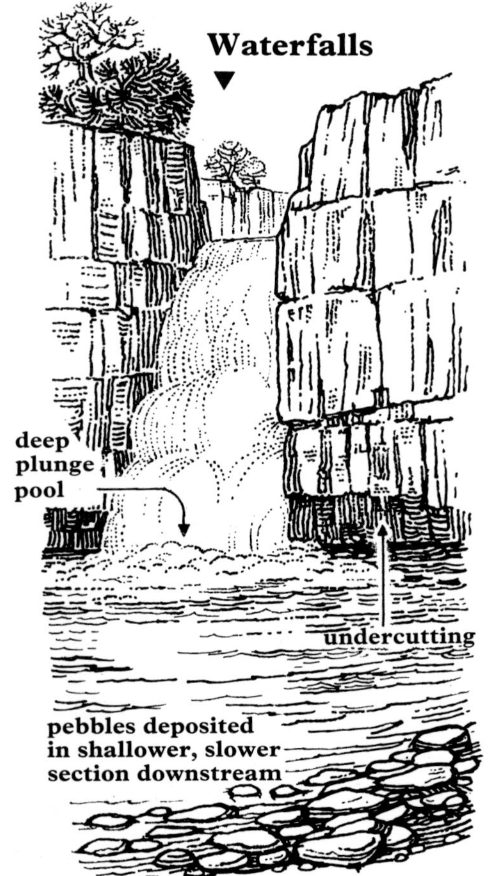

Meanders

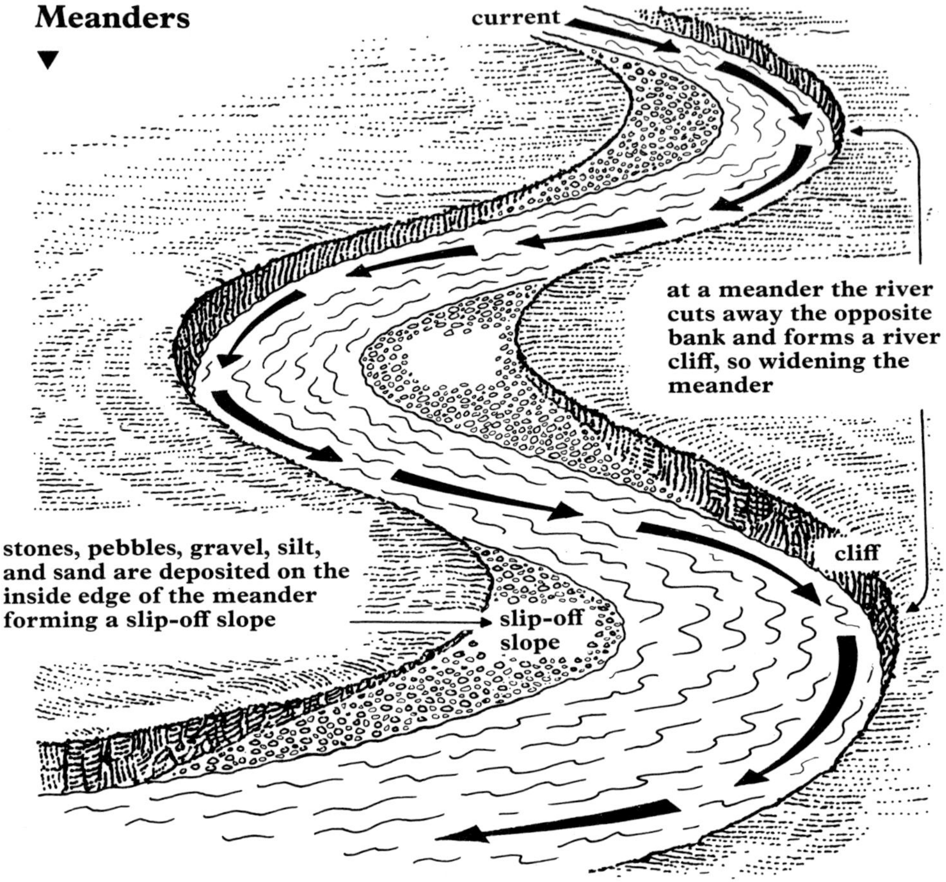

current
at a meander the river cuts away the opposite bank and forms a river cliff, so widening the meander
cliff
stones, pebbles, gravel, silt, and sand are deposited on the inside edge of the meander forming a slip-off slope
slip-off slope

Oxbow lakes

If a river continues to widen a meander, it reaches a point where a sudden flood will break through and cut off the meander, leaving it as a crescent of water called an **oxbow lake.**

1
2
3
4

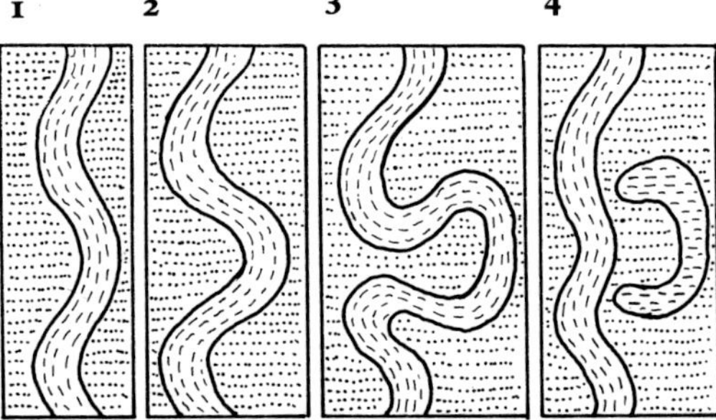

▲ **Potholes** are formed in solid bedrock. When a small waterfall is formed, it drops into a small plunge pool. The water in the pool spirals round under the force of the waterfall and as a result small stones at the bottom of the pool are swirled round too. In this way the action of the water drills holes in the stream bed.

▲ **Deltas** are only found in the British Isles where streams enter still lakes or still waters in a sea inlet. Sediment from the stream is deposited at the mouth of the stream and is not carried away by tidal action or by currents. In time it builds up a small area of land pushing out into the lake or sea inlet and forming the characteristic shape of a delta.

Terraces are formed where rivers cut down through their former flood plains to form new deeper courses. ▼

Flood plains are formed wherever a river floods regularly and deposits a coating of mud or silt on the floor of the valley. These coatings of mud add up to a considerable thickness of sediment with the passing of hundreds of years. The mud is always laid level so the characteristic feature of a river valley where the river floods regularly is the formation of a flat flood plain. Sometimes the deposits are of river gravel. ▼

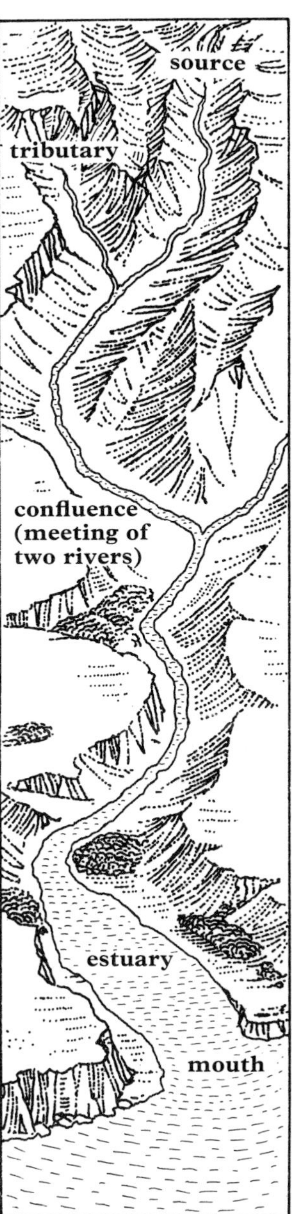

Trees in summer and winter

sweet
chestnut
lime
silver
birch
alder
larch
cedar
Douglas
fir
Scots
pine
yew

BRIDGES

▲ stepping stones

◀ **Stepping stones** are the simplest method of crossing a river apart from a **ford.**

▲ clapper bridge

A **slab bridge** is a simple bridge composed of a stone slab resting on supports on either side of the river, and ◀ a **clapper bridge** is just a series of slabs forming a continuous bridge.

▲ packhorse bridge

◀ **Packhorse bridges** were built to accommodate packhorses carrying goods. They are often narrow with quite a steep gradient to the top of the arch. They have a characteristic shape.

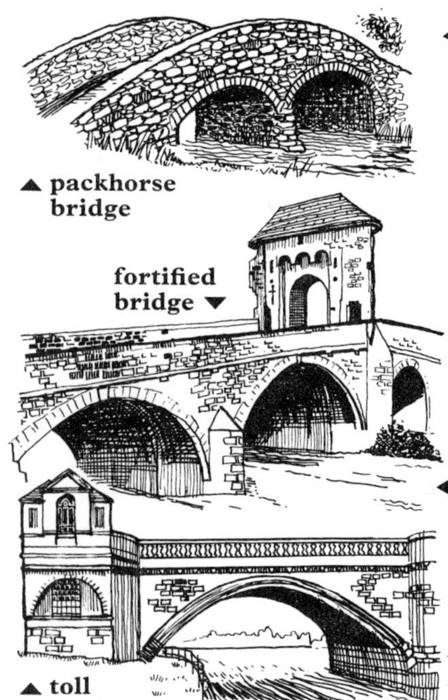

fortified bridge ▼

▲ toll bridge

Some bridges were **fortified** as at Monmouth and others carried **toll** ◀ **houses, chapels** and **houses.**

▼ cantilever bridge

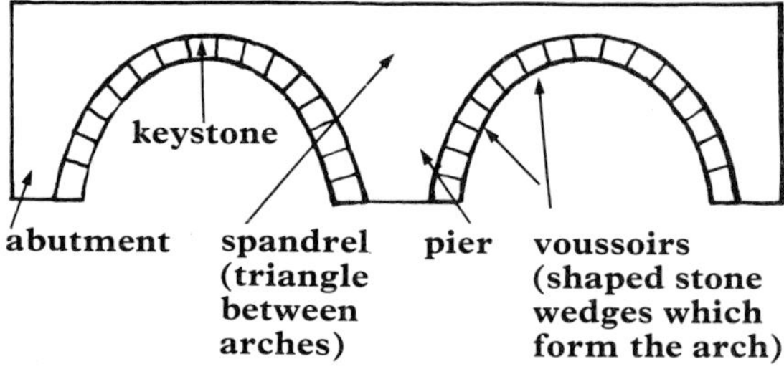

arch bridge ▶

The design of an **arch bridge** sometimes gives a clue to its age. A perfect **semi-circular arch** was typical of the eighteenth century. Other arch bridges tend to have arches somewhat similar to those fashionable in other buildings at the time (see pages 62–63). Modern **steel arch bridges** differ in design in that the routeway is usually suspended **from** the arch instead of going **over** the arch.

▼ iron arch bridge

◀ **Cantilever bridges** such as the Forth Bridge are based on the ingenious principle of counterbalancing forces.

Suspension bridges have high **towers** from which the bridge is suspended by means of **cables.** The cables are anchored to the land on either side of the bridge. Suspension bridges cost so much to build that they are rarely used over short distances.

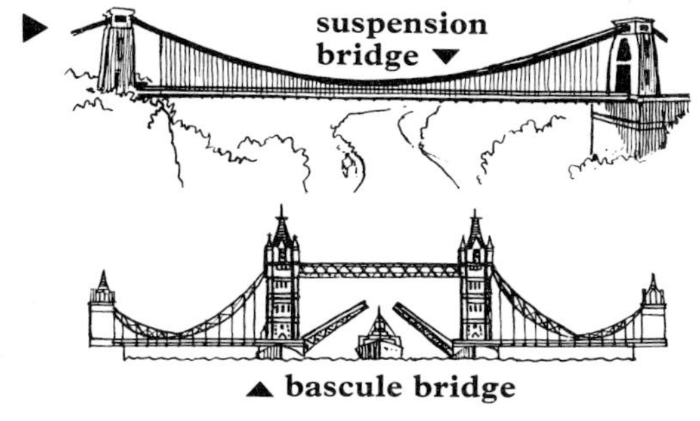

suspension bridge

bascule bridge

Bridges with moving parts include **bascule bridges** such as Tower Bridge, **transporter bridges** such as the bridge at Middlesbrough, **lift bridges** (often seen on **canals**) and **swing bridges** (often seen in **docks**).

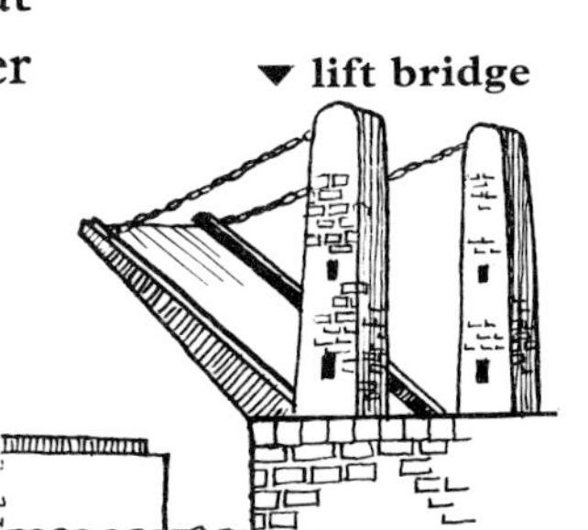

lift bridge

swing bridge

transporter bridge

Most modern bridges are **beam bridges** and follow the same basic principles as in the old slab bridge. **Girders** or **pre-stressed concrete beams** span the road, river or railway. These are relatively cheap and efficient ways of bridging short distances. Sometimes the beam bridge gains its strength from a **metal truss** which forms a distinctive, patterned **parapet** on either side of the bridge. **Bailey bridges** are temporary bridges erected by the army, often when the permanent bridge has been washed away. Sometimes bridges have been built over a line of boats (**pontoon bridges**).

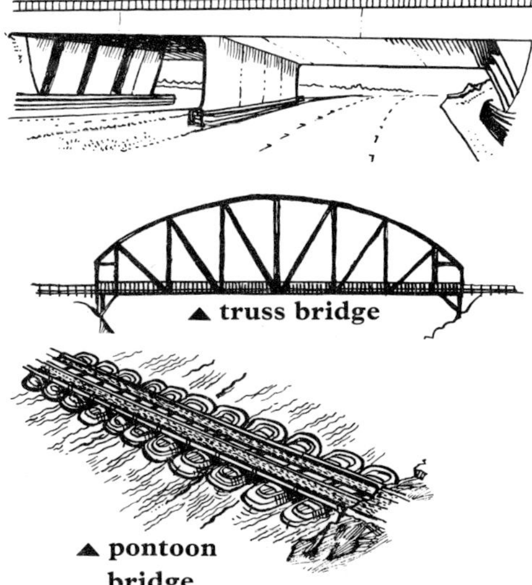

pre-stressed concrete bridge

truss bridge

pontoon bridge

FERRIES AND FORDS

At any major river or estuary it is usually possible to locate the site of a former **ferry** service used in the days before the erection of a bridge. Many ferries still operate, of course, particularly in highland areas. Many small streams were crossed in the past by means of **fords.** This can be seen from the large number of placenames ending in **ford** (Oxford, Brentford, Blandford, Orford, etc.).

WILD FLOWERS: SPRING AND SUMMER

These pictures show some of the commoner wild flowers of spring and early summer.

▼ primrose

▼ wood anemone

▼ bluebell

ragged robin ▼

▼ cowslip

◀ poppy

◀ violet

▲ field campion

◀ daffodil

◀ hedge parsley

◀ daisy

foxglove ▶

wild arum (lords and ladies) ▶

yellow iris ▶

WILD FLOWERS: AUTUMN AND WINTER

These pictures show some of the commoner wild flowers of late summer, autumn and winter.

AT THE ROADSIDE

Signposts, milestones, boundary stones, wayside crosses and **monuments** are some of the interesting features to be found at the roadside. Some signs (the **fingerpost signs**) have fingers on the ends pointing the way. Old milestones can sometimes be seen and there are examples of Roman milestones in Northumberland. Boundary stones such as the Three Shires Stone mark limits such as the meeting of county boundaries. There are monuments such as the **cross** marking the spot where the Battle of Towton was fought during the Wars of the Roses in the fifteenth century, or the **obelisk** at Northallerton marking a battleground where the Scots were beaten in the twelfth century.

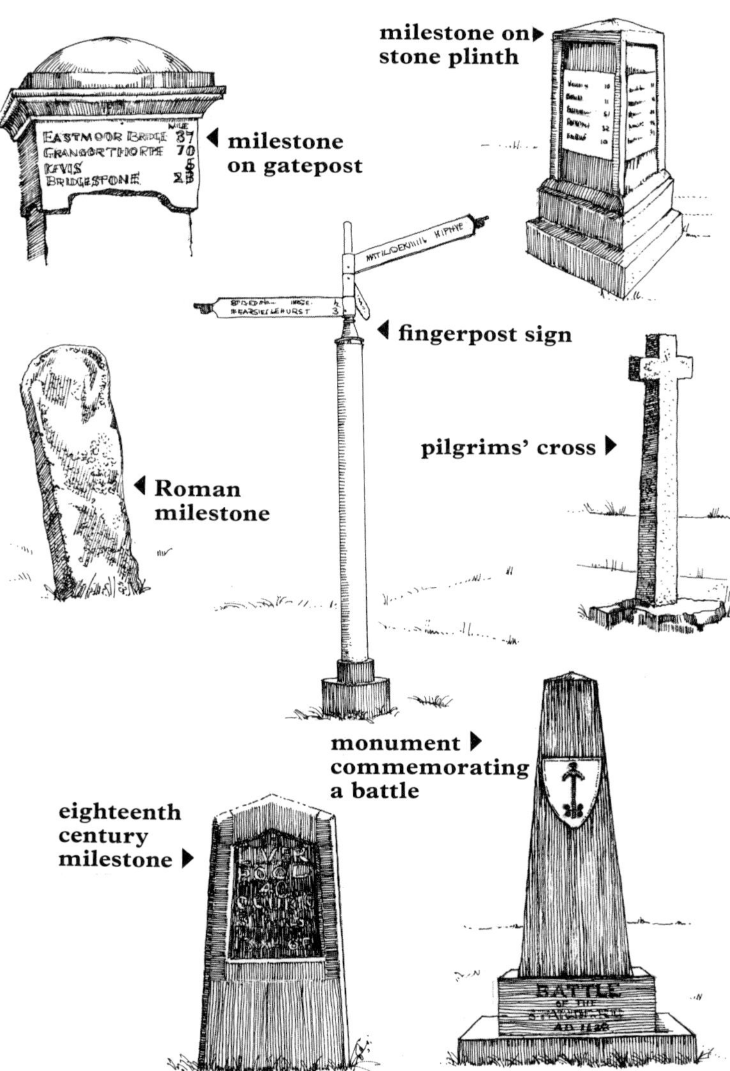

◀ cobbled pavement

Some **pavements** date back to medieval times. **Cobblestones** and well-worn **flagstones** are possible indicators of pavements which are over a hundred years or so old.

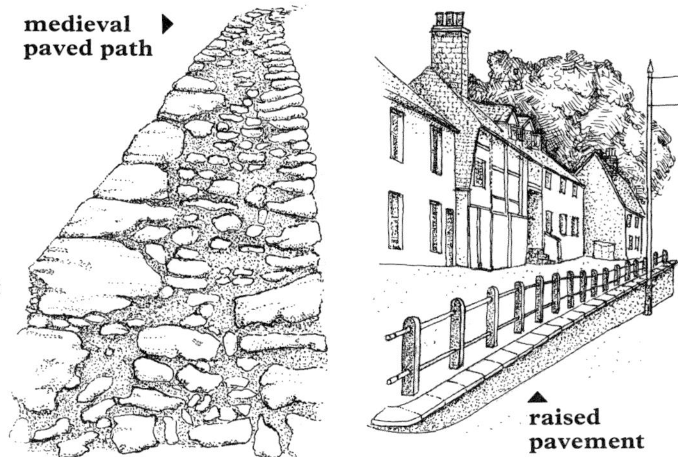

The days of horse-drawn vehicles can be recalled at many places from the **horse-troughs** at the sides of the roads. Other features which recall those days include **inn signs, coaching inns, mounting blocks, tethering posts,** etc. (see Alphabetical Index and Picture Index).

▲ **Road tunnels** are not as necessary as **rail tunnels,** because road vehicles can ascend steep gradients.

A COACHING INN

The coaching inns came to the fore in the peak period of coach travel from about 1750 to 1830.

A tunnel, sometimes called a **"porte-cochère",** allowed the coach to enter the inn **courtyard** from the main road. Inside passengers alighted there and were helped by attendants into the inn. Outside passengers who sat on the roof and paid roughly half price for their tickets often had to alight in the main road before the coach went under the tunnel or arch.

The inn courtyard had **stables** for the horses and **storehouses** of fodder and necessary items of equipment for servicing the coaches. There was often a **gallery** running round the sides of the courtyard at first floor level.

tunnel

INN SIGNS

The pictures on this page show just a few of the hundreds of inn signs of the British Isles. Many inn signs throw light on the life of the people of a district such as "The Woolpack" in an old textile town, "The Traveller's Rest" on a former routeway and "The Plough" in a farming district.

Many inn signs recall great events of the past or famous people.

Sometimes the name of a hotel or public house is shown by a statue or model rather than by a painted inn sign, such as the "Woolpack" inn on page 34, or an actual bell ("Bell" Inn), a wooden animal (e.g. "White Bull") or even a beehive.

▲ royalty ▲

▲ animals

▲ heraldry

▲ war

▲ crafts and industries

▲ farming

▲ events

▲ unusual signs—this one "The Goat and Compasses" used to be "God encompasseth us"

▲ sports

RED ROSE

▲ emblems

▲ famous people

ROADS OF THE PAST

Roads are the essential features of any civilisation. Even in prehistoric times there were **trackways.** Some of these still exist to this day.

▼ **prehistoric trackway**

Other roads take peculiar roundabout courses because they follow old **boundaries.** Often paths and roads recall specific trade routes such as the **drove roads** which were used when herds of animals were taken across country, or the aptly named **salt ways** used by the salt merchants. **Green lanes** are country paths which have not been surfaced.

▼ **green lane**

In Devon and Cornwall paths often appear as **sunken lanes** with steep **earth banks** and **hedges** on either side. The lanes have literally sunk with the passage of time.

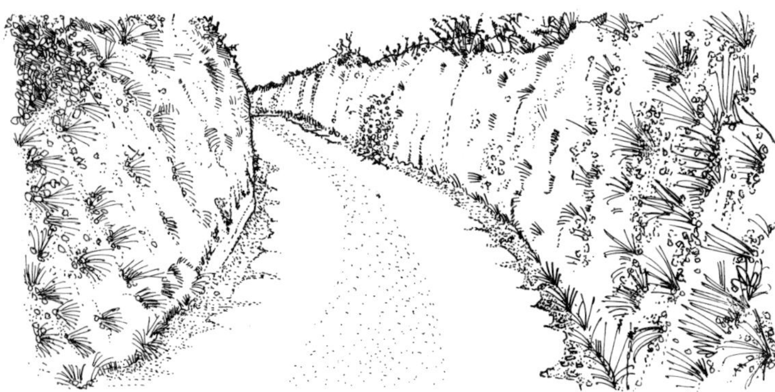

▲ **sunken lane**

Packhorse routes can sometimes be traced on either side of a packhorse bridge. A stone **"causey"** or **causeway** was sometimes built to enable the paths to be used in all weathers.

▲ **causeway**

TURNPIKES

The greatest road building programme since the time of the Romans was initiated in the eighteenth century with the building of **turnpike roads.** These were roads built by turnpike trusts. They maintained the roads and paid for them out of tolls which they charged. Consequently they built **toll bars** and **toll houses** where the tollkeeper collected the money. The routes they followed can be located on old maps. Sometimes the turnpike route can be followed by locating old **coaching** inns which may stand now on what appear to be side roads. Sometimes old toll houses still remain in good condition to remind us of this period of history and sometimes as at Hunter's Bar in Sheffield we are even reminded of the barriers across what used to be the road.

▲ **old map showing turnpike ("T. Pike") north-east of "SOUTHAMPTON"**

▲ **Hunter's Bar**

◀ **tollhouse**

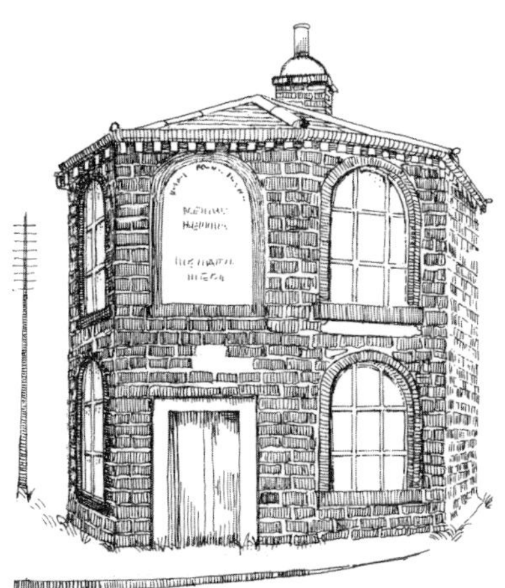
tollhouse ▶

ROAD SIGNS

As a general rule:

Red circles are used for signs which prohibit.

▲ No entry

▲ No right turn

▲ No left turn

▲ No U-turn

▲ Overtaking prohibited

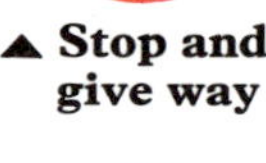

▲ Stop and give way

▲ No waiting

▲ No stopping (Clearway)

▲ Give way to vehicles from opposite direction

▲ All motor vehicles prohibited

▲ Buses and coaches prohibited

▲ Lorries prohibited

▲ Cycle and moped riding prohibited

▲ No pedestrians

▲ limited to maximum speed permitted for type of road

▲ Maximum speed limit

Blue circles are used for signs which give orders.

▲ Minimum speed limit

▲ End of minimum speed limit

▲ Ahead only

▲ Turn left

▲ Turn left ahead

▲ Keep left

▲ Pass either side

▲ Route for cyclists and moped riders (compulsory)

▲ roundabout circulation

Red triangles warn of dangers ahead.

▲ Cross roads
Roundabout ▼
▲ T junction
Staggered junction ▼
▲ Side road
Bend to right ▼
▲ Double bend first to left
Series of bends ▼
▲ Two-way traffic straight ahead
Two-way traffic crosses one-way road ▼

▲ Traffic merges from left
Traffic joins from right ▼
▲ Road narrows on both sides
Steep hill downward ▼
▲ Steep hill upwards
Children ▼
▲ Pedestrian crossing
Traffic signals ▼
▲ Hump bridge
Uneven road ▼

▲ Road works
Change to opposite carriageway ▼
▲ Right hand lane closed
Horses and ponies ▼
▲ Cattle
Wild animals ▼
▲ Level crossing with automatic half-barriers ahead
Level crossing with other barrier or gate ahead ▼
▲ Level crossing without gate or barrier ahead

▲ Slippery road
Opening or swing bridge ▼
▲ Quayside or river bank
Worded warning sign ▼
Ford
▲ Falling or fallen rock
Low-flying aircraft or sudden aircraft noise ▼

Red triangles upside down warn of main roads ahead.

GIVE WAY

◀ Give way to traffic on major road

Forton Services

▲ Direction to service area with fuel, parking, cafeteria and restaurant facilities

▲ One-way traffic

One-way street ▼

ONE WAY

▲ Priority over vehicles from opposite direction

▲ No through road

▲ Advance warning of no through road

◀ Parking place—plate indicates lorry park

Hospital

Hospital

MOTORWAYS AND ROAD VEHICLES

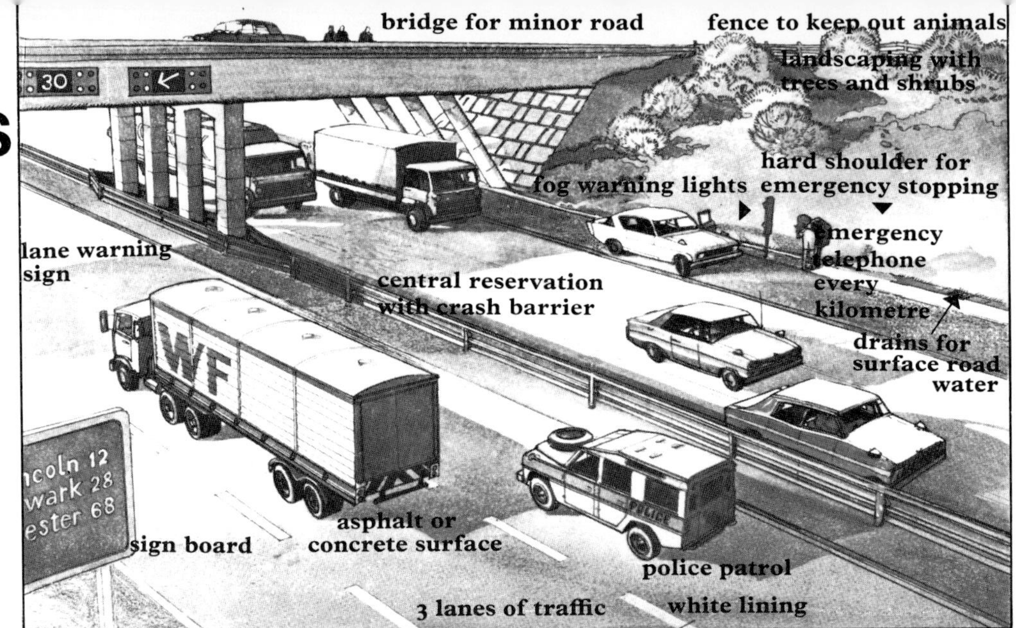

hopper

pick-up truck

pantechnicon

tractor and trailer

articulated lorry

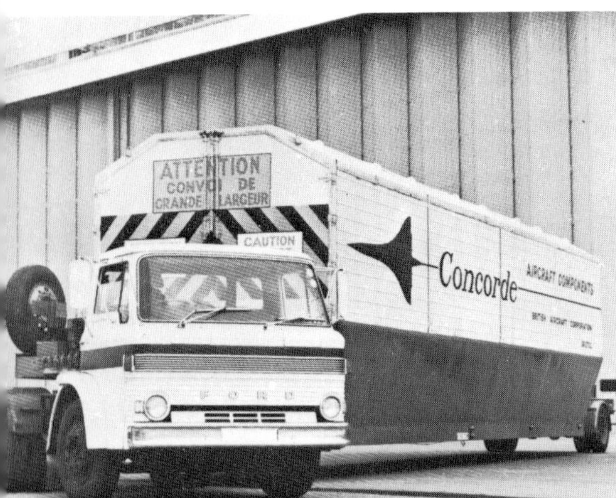

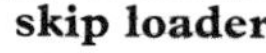

skip loader

breakdown truck

flour tanker

crane carrier

car transporter

light van

fuel tanker

ROAD WORKS

These pictures show some of the heavy vehicles you may see wherever a new road is being constructed. The **Crawler Dozer, Crawler Excavator** and **Face Shovel** scoop and dig and prepare the site. They fill the **Dump Trucks** which are specially designed to carry very heavy loads over rough uneven surfaces. The **Scraper** and **Grader** level the site by scraping out uneven hummocks and putting earth in the hollows. The **Roller** finishes off the work of preparing the ground for the men who will apply a thick layer of concrete to the surface or finish it with asphalt.

backacter (another kind of excavator)

sheep's foot rollers

scraper

REGISTRATION LETTERS

The place of origin of a coach or lorry can usually be identified from the name of the town or village printed on the side of the vehicle. The place of origin of a car can sometimes be guessed at from the car registration letters. Each combination of letters is normally reserved for use by a particular district in the British Isles. The last two letters denote the authority which first registered the vehicle. These can be looked up in a list such as that published in the A.A. Handbook. Thus the number BNG 123M indicates that the car was registered in Norfolk.

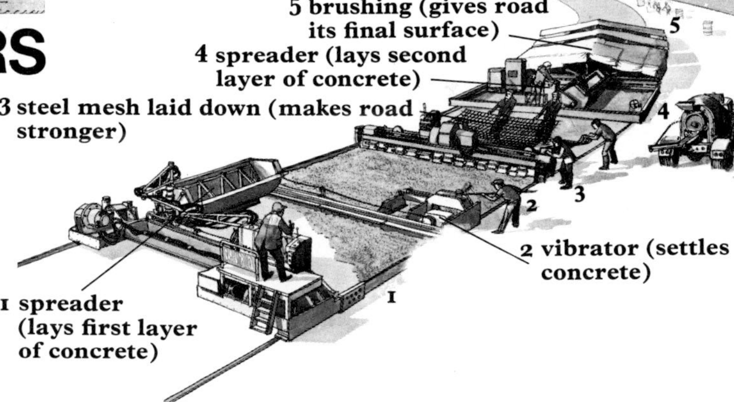

There are certain patterns in the combinations which it may be useful to note:

1) All containing an S are from Scotland.

2) All containing an I or a Z are from Ireland.

CANALS

1
lock gate A
lock gate B
boat
LOCK
lower water level
higher water level
2
water level lowered by opening sluice on gate A
3
lock filled by opening sluice on B—
boat lifted to higher level

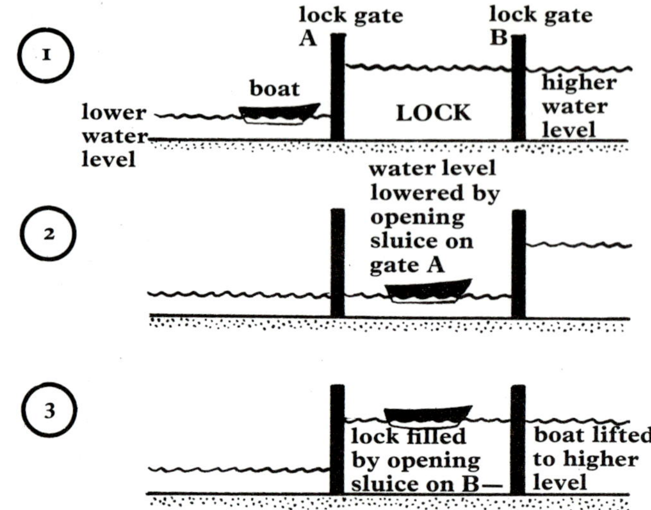

Canals were dug mainly between 1760 and 1830. Although their importance for the transport of heavy goods has declined ever since the coming of the railways over 140 years ago, they have tended to remain as canals because it often costs more to fill them in than to maintain them. Today they are often used by pleasure boats. Many of the features shown in these pictures can be seen in the course of a walk of a few kilometres along the **towpath** of many canals.

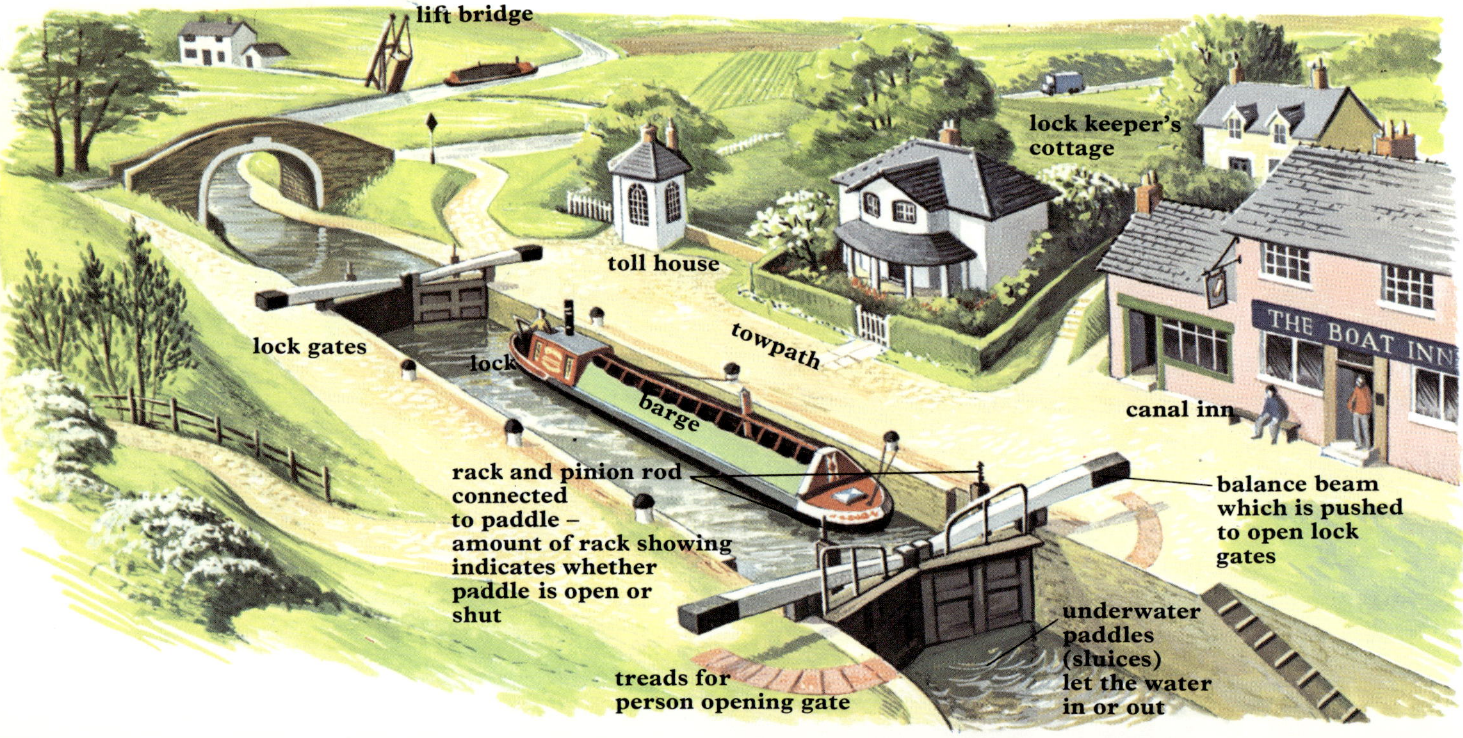

lift bridge
lock keeper's cottage
toll house
lock gates
towpath
lock
barge
THE BOAT INN
canal inn
rack and pinion rod connected to paddle – amount of rack showing indicates whether paddle is open or shut
balance beam which is pushed to open lock gates
underwater paddles (sluices) let the water in or out
treads for person opening gate

▲ boat emerging from a tunnel

▲ canalside factory

▲ a flight of locks, taking the canal up or down a hill side—sometimes they are so close together that boats move from one lock straight into the next, then known as "staircase locks"

▲ working boat

the Anderton lift used to lift even large boats mechanically from one level to the next ▶

a lock and lock keeper's cottage ▼

RAILWAYS

The railways are changing. Many features such as **semaphore signals** are being replaced. Steam engines have gone, new rolling stock has appeared to cope with containers, new lines are being electrified. Even the sounds of the railway are disappearing. The **continuously welded** track of today eliminates the familiar "clickety-clack" of the train journey.

▼ coal wagons ▼ ▼ timber wagon ▼ refrigeration wagon

▲ cattle wagon ▲ road vehicle trailer ▲ container wagons

◀ rail tank for bulk liquids

hopper for bulk solids ▶

low-loader with a dropped middle for extra high loads ▶

Containers of a standard size are often used in industry today to speed up the delivery of goods. Mechanical handling ensures that goods are loaded swiftly from lorry to railway to ship.

two-aspect electric signal ▼

◀ pantograph on locomotive taking electricity from the contact wire

▲ marshalling yard (sidings)

shunting locomotive ▶

RAILWAY SIGNALS AND SIGNS

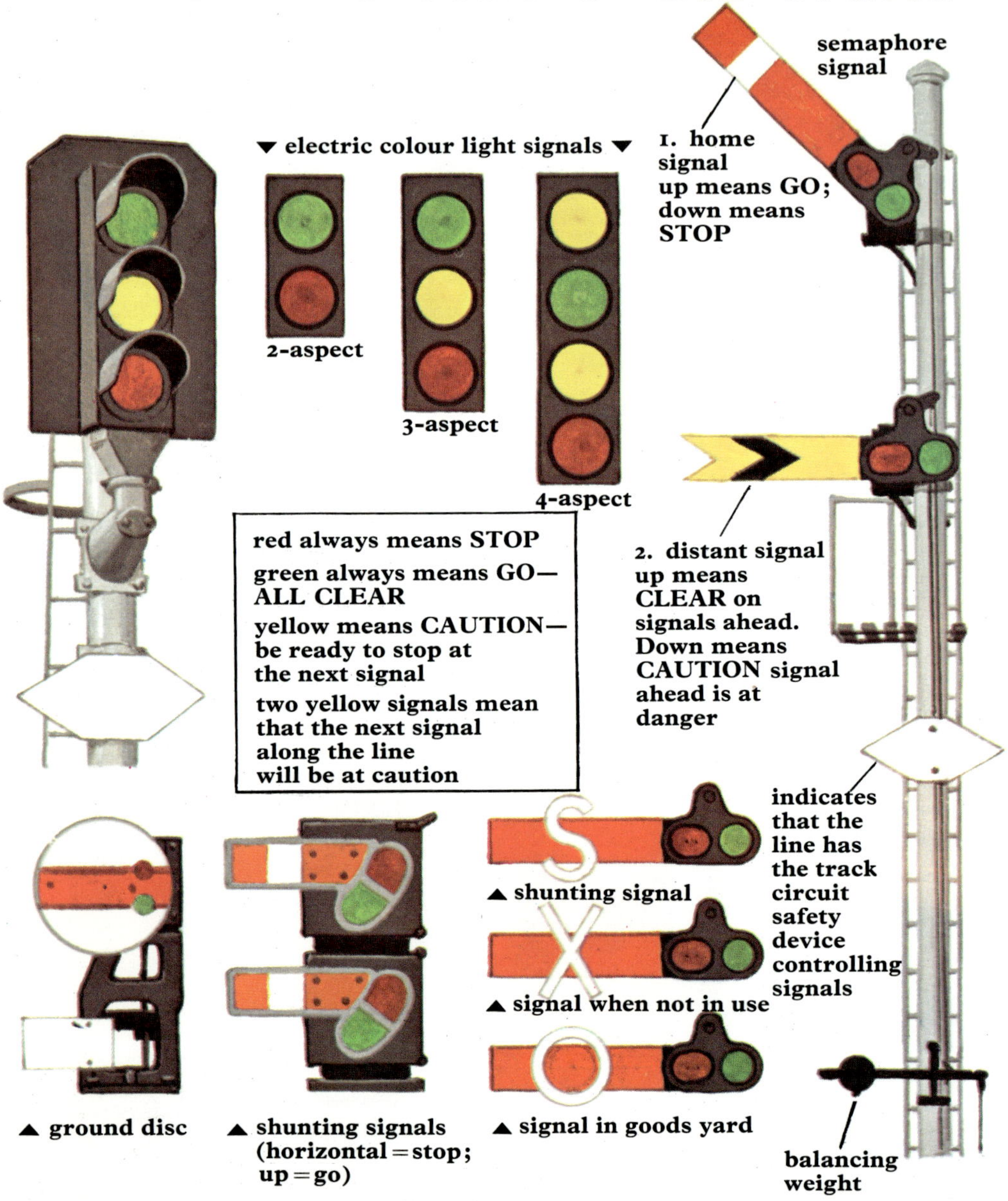

▼ electric colour light signals ▼

2-aspect

3-aspect

4-aspect

red always means STOP

green always means GO—ALL CLEAR

yellow means CAUTION—be ready to stop at the next signal

two yellow signals mean that the next signal along the line will be at caution

semaphore signal

1. home signal up means GO; down means STOP

2. distant signal up means CLEAR on signals ahead. Down means CAUTION signal ahead is at danger

indicates that the line has the track circuit safety device controlling signals

balancing weight

▲ ground disc

▲ shunting signals (horizontal = stop; up = go)

▲ shunting signal

▲ signal when not in use

▲ signal in goods yard

Relics of former days can be seen on most railway routes. **Notices** warning would-be trespassers often carry the imprint of the **old railway company** (such as the L.N.E.R. or even earlier such as the Furness Railway). At railway stations the **signal box, booking office, waiting rooms** and other station buildings, the **railway inn** or **hotel** outside and the **street names** all recall the heyday of the railways.

distance posts
(to the next station) ▼

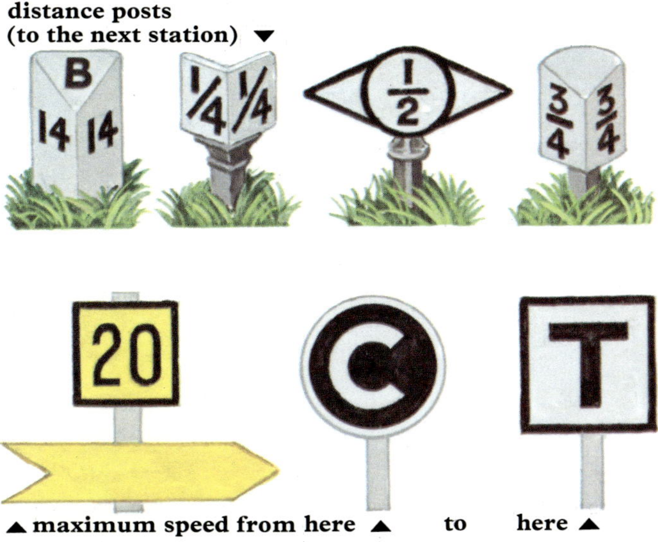

▲ maximum speed from here ▲ to here ▲

pointing down
= down hill

▲ old boundary post

▲ gradient post (in this case indicating a downhill slope of 1 in 146); pointing up = uphill

The **yellow front** of a train makes it conspicuous to the men who work on the railway track. They wear **orange waistcoats** to make them conspicuous to engine drivers.

▲ warns engine driver to whistle

▲ continuous welded track

DESPOILING THE LANDSCAPE

▼ dump

▼ colliery tip

▼ quarry

Ugliness is everywhere. **Spoil heaps** due to the extraction of minerals often spoil the appearance of the countryside as do corporation **rubbish tips** which have not been hidden from the eye. Many people object to other features in the countryside such as lines of **pylons,** badly-sited **caravan sites,** new **motorways, aerials** and other **towers.**

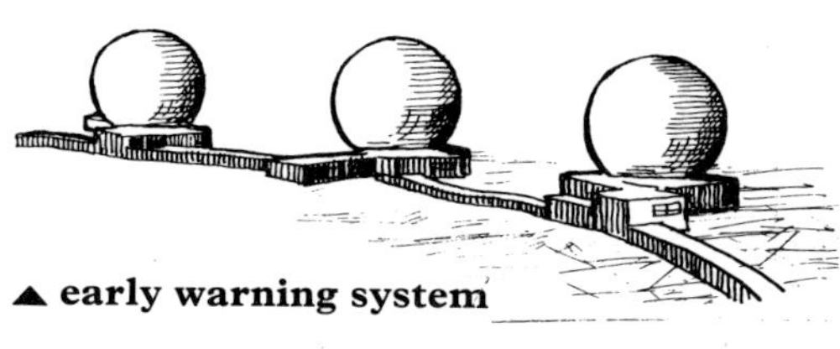

▲ early warning system

telegraph pole ▶

▲ electricity pylons ▼

electricity supply line to farm ▼

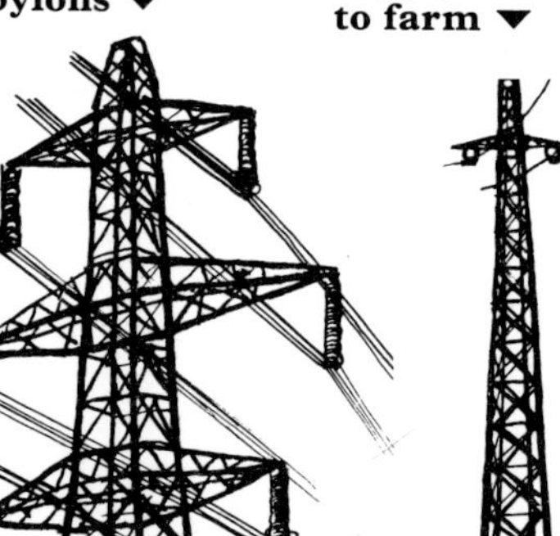

▼ TV aerial

TV and radio masts ▼

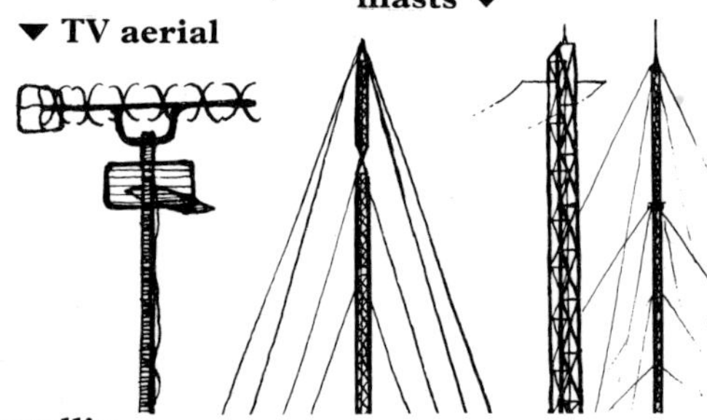

satellite communications centre ▶

▲ radio telescope

COAST

PANORAMA: THE COAST

cliffs
stacks
caves
lighthouse
headland
coastguard
station
groynes
dunes

COASTAL FEATURES

▲ **Sand dunes** are formed at beaches where fresh sand is regularly deposited by the sea. Wind picks up drying sand at low tide and blows it inland. Nowadays this drifting sand is caught by planting **marram grass** in a bed of **pine branches. Pine forests** are also planted as a further deterrent.

▲ **Beach channels** often break up otherwise flat beaches. At high tide they present something of a trap to unwary bathers who cannot swim.

▲ **Saltings** are the marshland areas half-sea and half-land to be found in many coastal areas, especially where the sea is depositing sand or silt.

▲ **Sea walls** are necessary in many areas to protect the cliffs from being eroded by the waves (see pages 142–143).

▲ **Raised beaches** are former beaches left high and dry today because the sea level has fallen in those areas.

▲ **Groynes** are erected out of wood or concrete to hold sand or shingle drifting alongshore. The direction in which the sand is drifting can easily be seen merely by inspecting the groynes and seeing against which side the sand or shingle is heaped up.

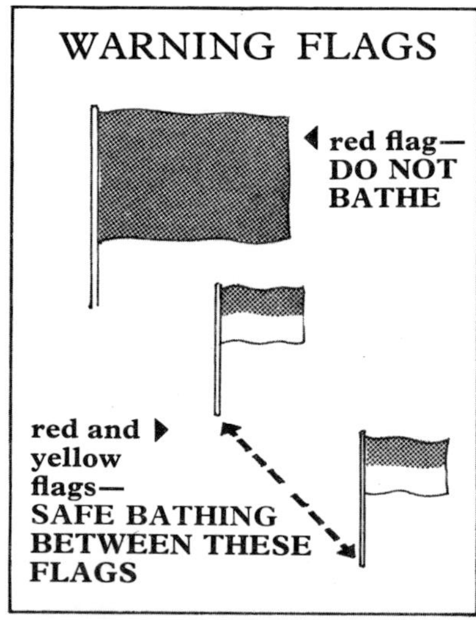

FIORDS

These are glacial valleys (see pages 102–103) at the coast. When the sea level rose (due to the melting of the ice caps) these U-shaped valleys were flooded. As a result the erosive effects of ice on the floor of the valley cannot be seen, but often large drumlins and terminal moraines appear above the surface of the water as **islands.** Fiords are known as **sea lochs** in Scotland.

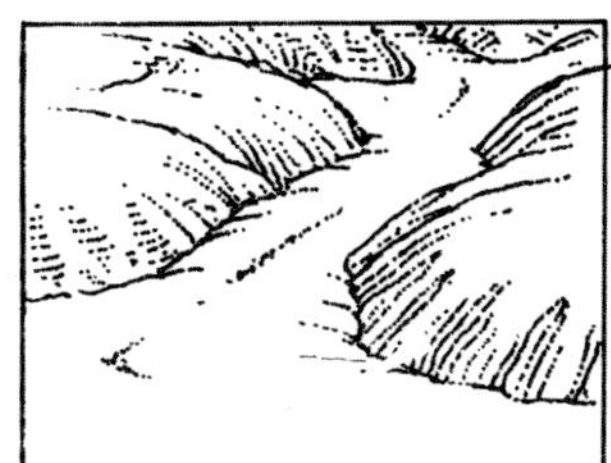

glacier in valley

ice melts and valley floods with sea water

▼ Loch Leven, Scotland

RIAS

These are normal river valleys (see pages 110–111) which were flooded due to a rise in sea-level. They appear on a map as long winding inlets with many branches. They fill with water at high tide. At low tide many **mud banks** appear.

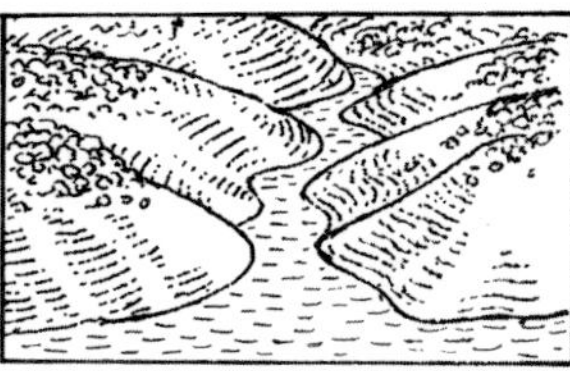

normal river valley

wide estuary as sea level rises

▼ St. Just, Cornwall

SEASHORE CREATURES

These pictures show some of the creatures likely to be found living between the low tide and high tide levels or to have been washed there by the waves.

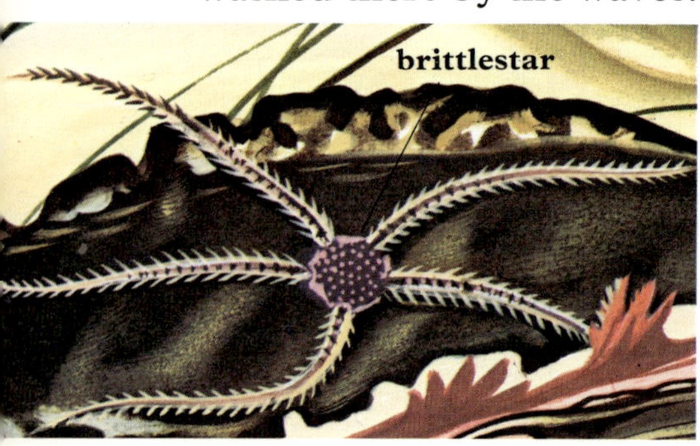

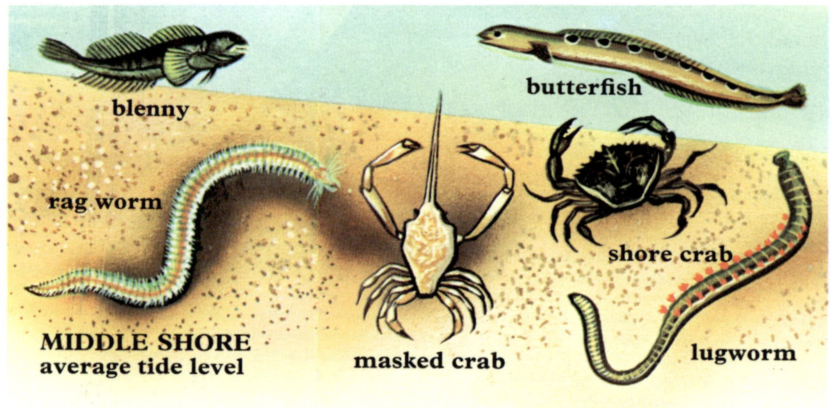

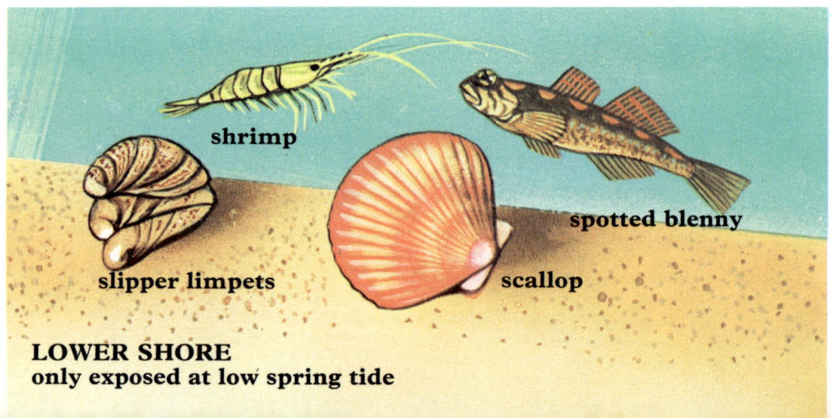

A ROCK POOL

shrimp

common blenny

two kinds of plumrose anemones

dahlia anemone

sea urchin

opelet or snakelocks anemone

common starfish

hermit crab

crab

CLIFF FEATURES

Stacks are small pinnacles or islands of rock close to the cliff edge. They used to be part of the cliff, but wave erosion has separated them from the headland.

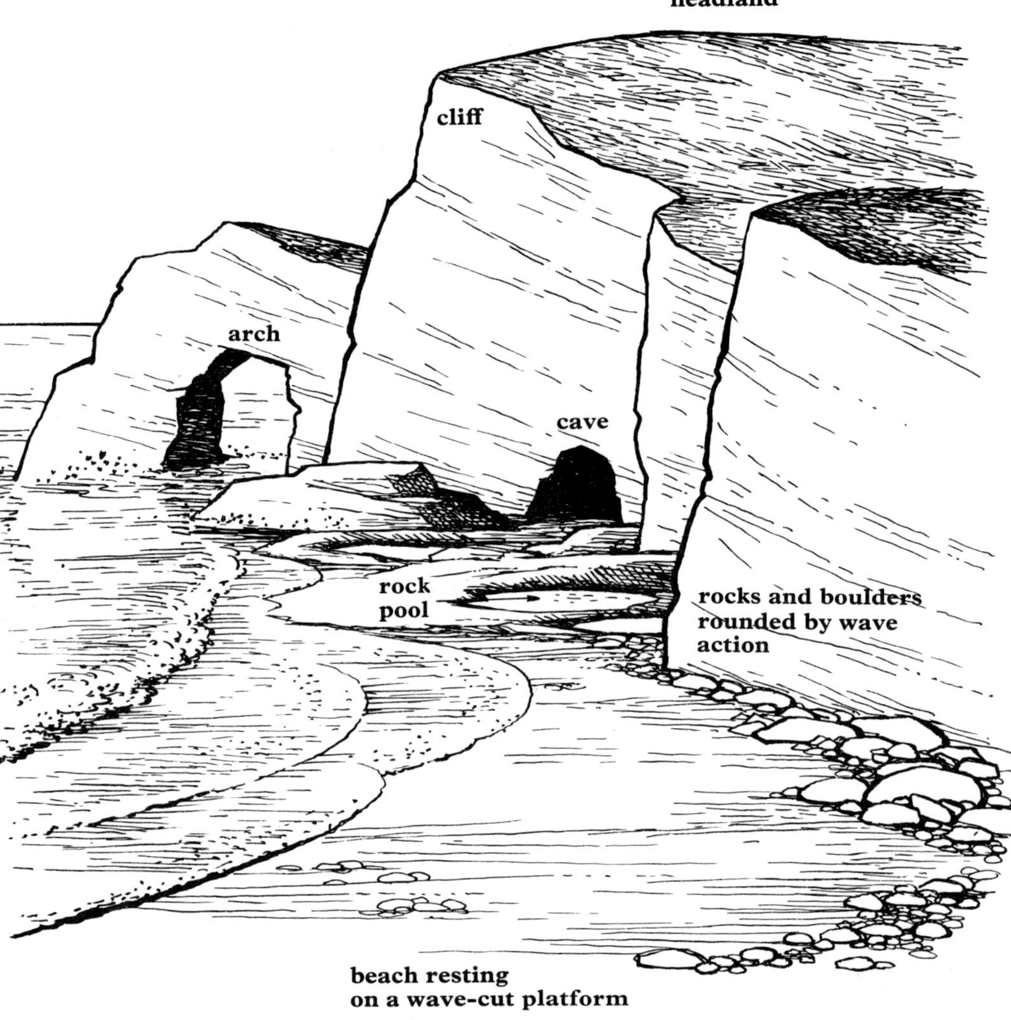

Caves are usually formed where there is a line of weakness in the rocks. Softer rocks are dislodged and constant erosion carves a hole which widens and deepens to become a cave. In time this process may cause the sea to break right through the cave leaving behind an **arch.**

▲

Cliffs are formed where hills reach the edge of the sea. Wave action throws stones at the base of the cliff. In hard rocks **notches** are formed, in soft rocks the base of the cliff is **undermined** and **collapses.** The shape of the cliff depends on the hardness and type of the cliff rock. Soft rocks **slump** while very hard rocks may even **overhang.**

Notches can be seen at the base of a cliff where the rock is hard and rugged. They are rounded and smoothed by waves throwing pebbles at them. In time the notches develop into **caves** and **arches.**

▼

▲

Wavecut platform is the name given to the beach at the base of a cliff which has been eroded or cut by the waves. This is where the old cliffs used to stand and which have since been eroded away by the sea. Since the wave action is always at the high tide level, the platform left behind always tends to be flat.

SHELLS

There are many different types of shell. These pictures help to identify the main varieties.

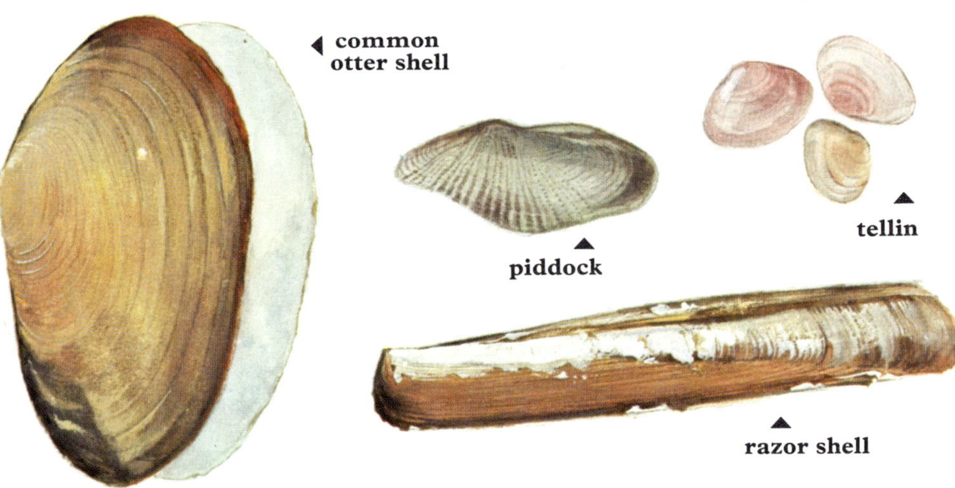

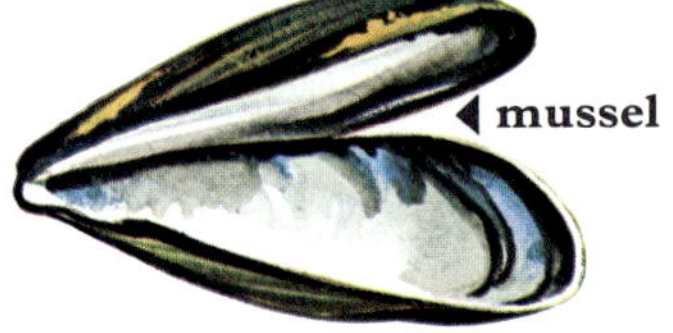

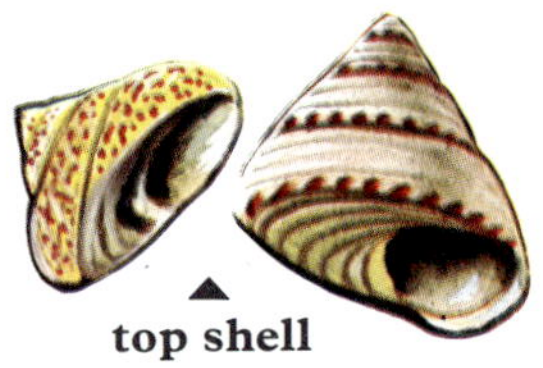

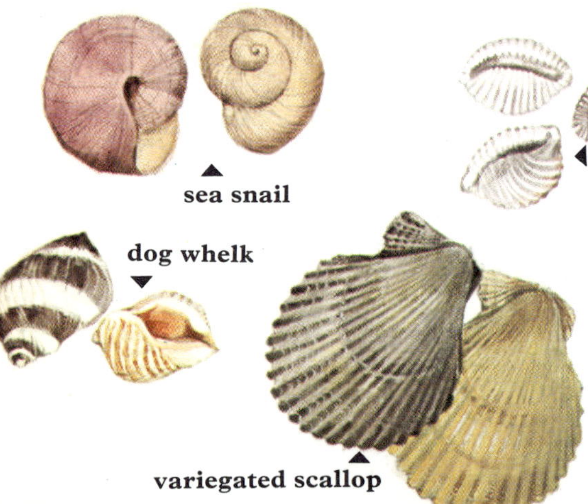

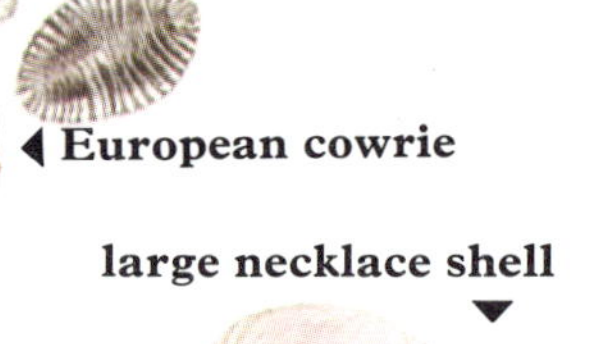

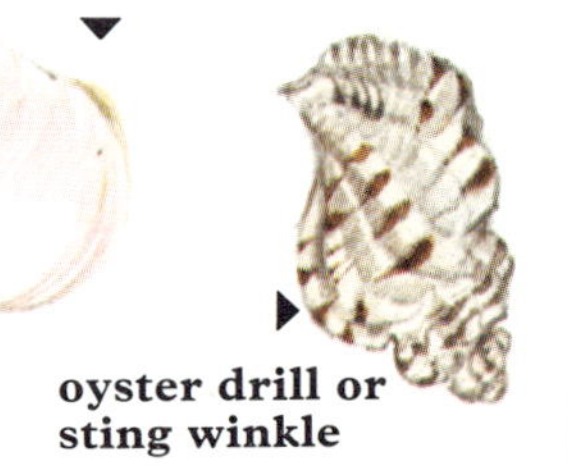

auger shell

flat winkle

SEAWEEDS

These are the most common types of seaweeds to be found between the low tide and high tide levels.

A PORT

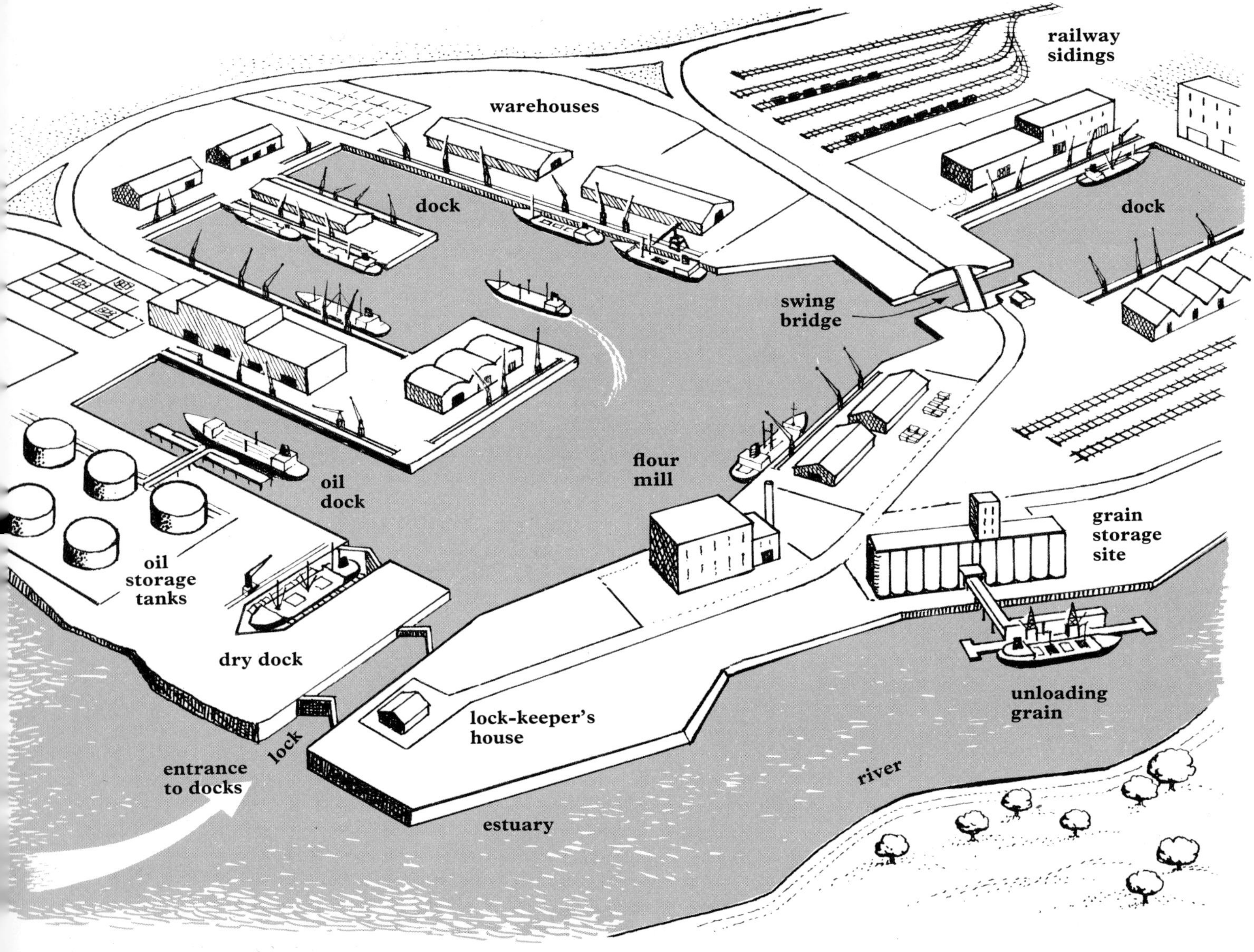

warehouses
railway sidings
dock
dock
swing bridge
oil dock
flour mill
grain storage site
oil storage tanks
dry dock
lock-keeper's house
unloading grain
lock
entrance to docks
river
estuary

PORT FEATURES

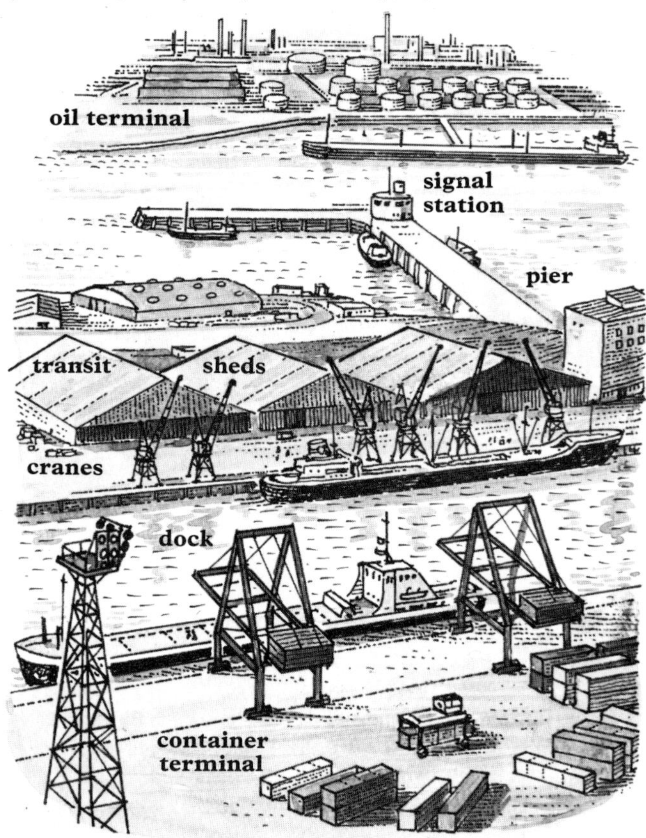

Some ports are situated on a river and use **quays** on the banks and **special docks** for berthing ships. Some seaports are situated where **jetties** or **piers** have created artificial harbours or improved existing natural features. Some ports have grown up round a **canal.** Most major seaports are situated on the **estuaries** of the great rivers.

PORTS IN THE PAST

Old warehouses are often to be seen, particularly those of the Hanseatic League of the fifteenth and sixteenth centuries.

▲ sixteenth century warehouses

▲ nineteenth century warehouses

In some ports there are unusual features such ◀ as this **look-out tower** at King's Lynn used by a merchant to watch for his ships coming up the River Ouse.

Old ports often have **customs houses** and ▶ other administrative buildings associated with the port in the past.

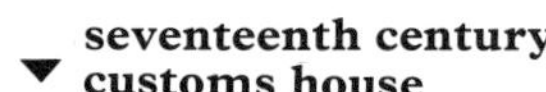

▼ seventeenth century customs house

TYPES OF SHIPS

These pictures show some of the principal types of ships using ports today.

▲ passenger liner

▲ dry bulker (e.g. coal, iron ore)

▲ oil tanker

▲ cargo/passenger liner

▲ container ship

▲ general cargo vessel

▲ car ferry

▲ hydrofoil

▲ hovercraft

FLAGS

These pictures identify many of the flags you will see flying from the masts of ships in harbour, or entering or leaving port.

navigation lights at night seen from straight ahead

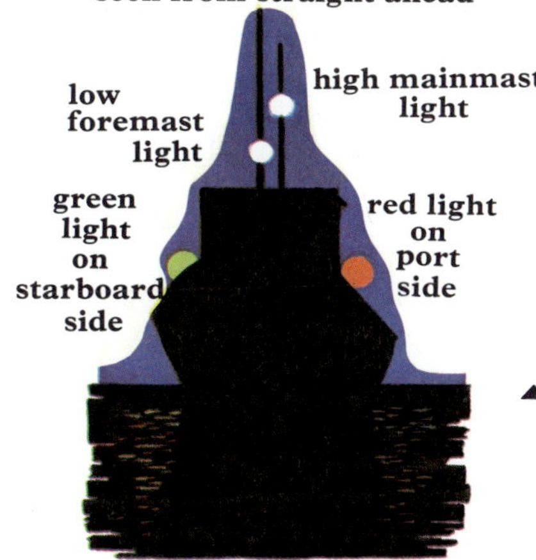

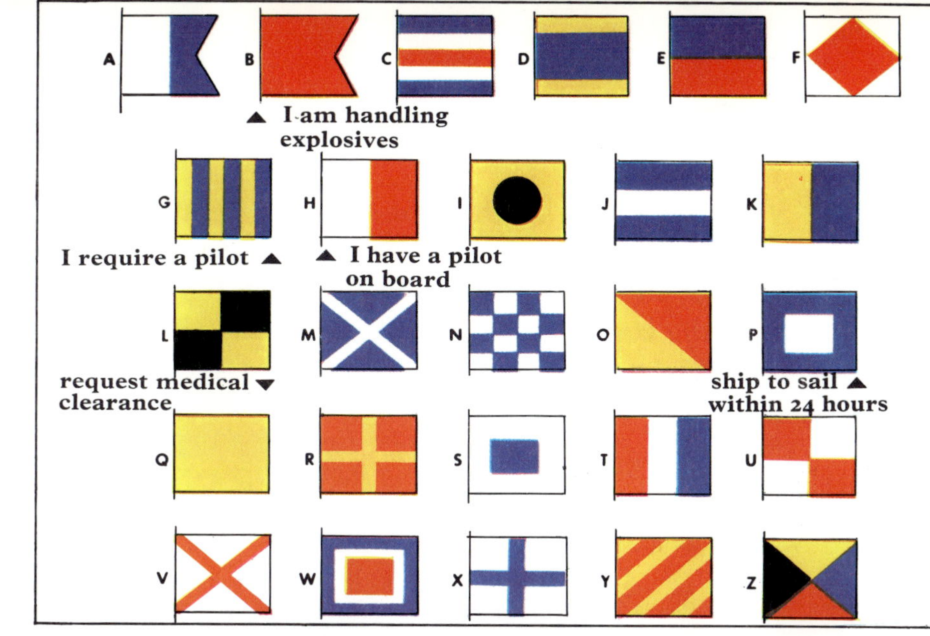

▲ White Ensign—the Royal Navy and the Royal Yacht Squadron

▲ Blue Ensign—the Royal Naval Reserve

▲ Red Ensign—the British Merchant Navy

▲ Royal Fleet Auxiliary

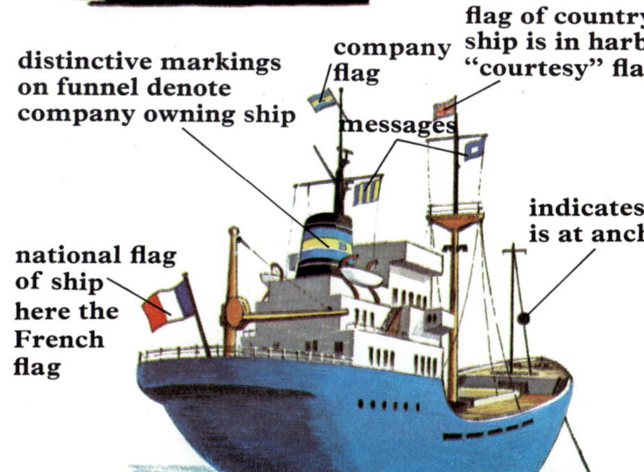

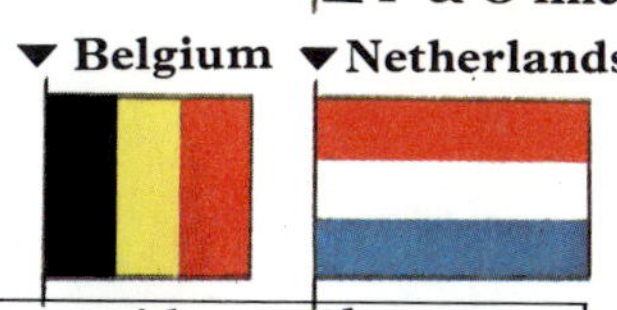

▲ P & O line

H.M. Customs

▼ Belgium

▼ Netherlands

LIGHTHOUSES

The idea of having a light on shore or on rocks to guide or warn ships dates back to antiquity as you can see from the pictures on the opposite page showing Roman and medieval lighthouses. At most places on the coast it is difficult to travel far without seeing a **lighthouse. Lightships** and **light towers** are usually some distance offshore.

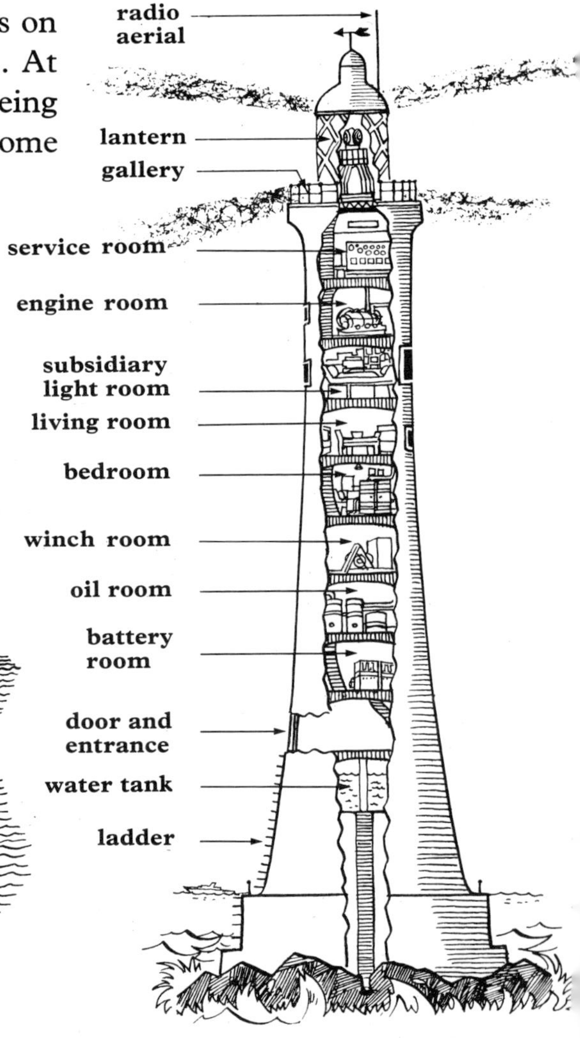

radio aerial
lantern
gallery
service room
engine room
subsidiary light room
living room
bedroom
winch room
oil room
battery room
door and entrance
water tank
ladder

lighthouse ▲

light tower ▼

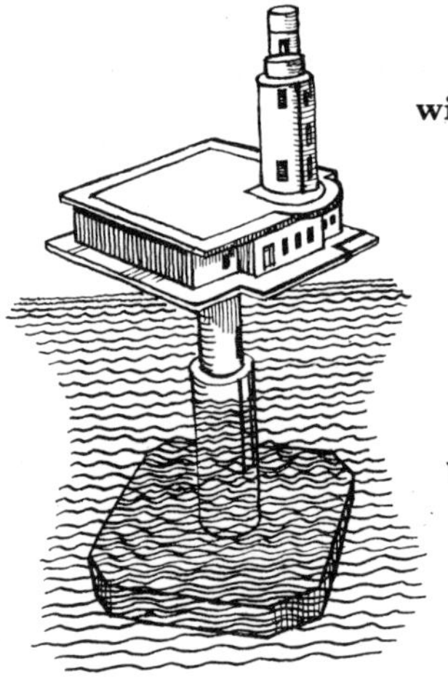

lightship ▼

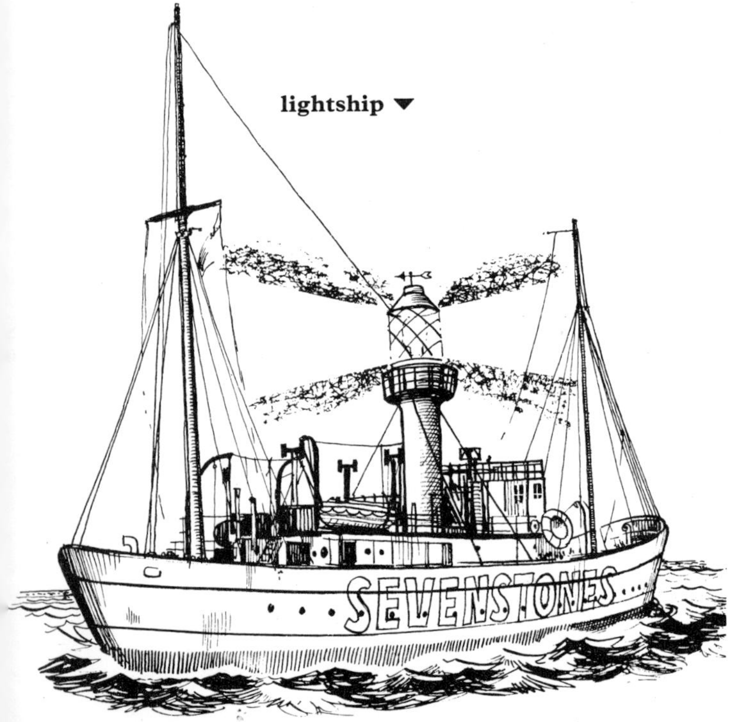

SEVENSTONES

LIGHTHOUSES OF THE PAST

▲ Roman lighthouse

▲ medieval lighthouse

▲ Winstanley's lighthouse, 1698

COASTGUARD STATIONS

These are primarily concerned these days with taking action when ships get into trouble offshore or whenever some other coastal emergency occurs.

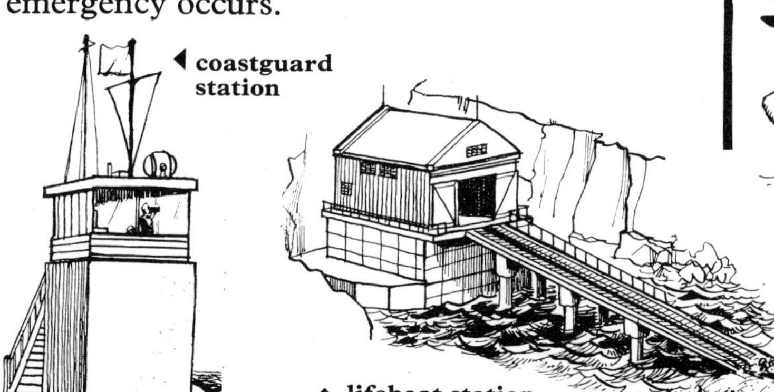

◀ coastguard station

▲ lifeboat station

LIFEBOAT STATIONS

Lifeboat stations are run by the Royal National Lifeboat Institution. A number of different types of lifeboats are used as you can see from these pictures. The **inshore boat** is used primarily for bathers, yachts, rowing boats and other craft in difficulty fairly close to the shore.

coastguard boat ▼

▲ inshore boat

▼ lifeboat

A FISHING PORT

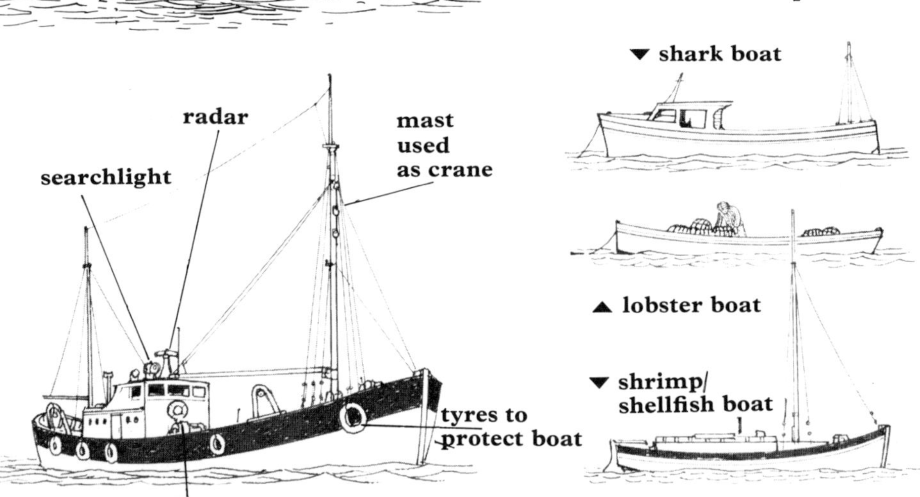

BOATS AND METHODS

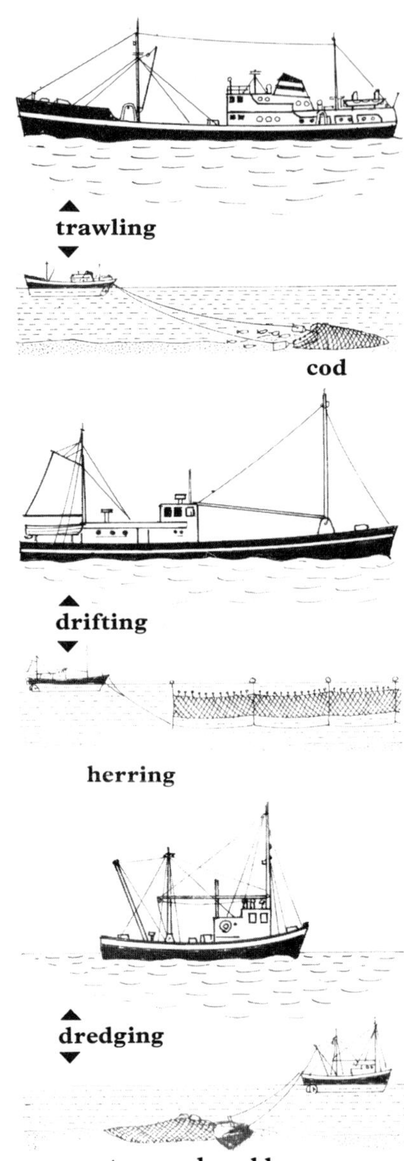

HARBOUR FEATURES

Kippering kilns

These are the buildings where herrings are smoked and processed to become kippers. ▼

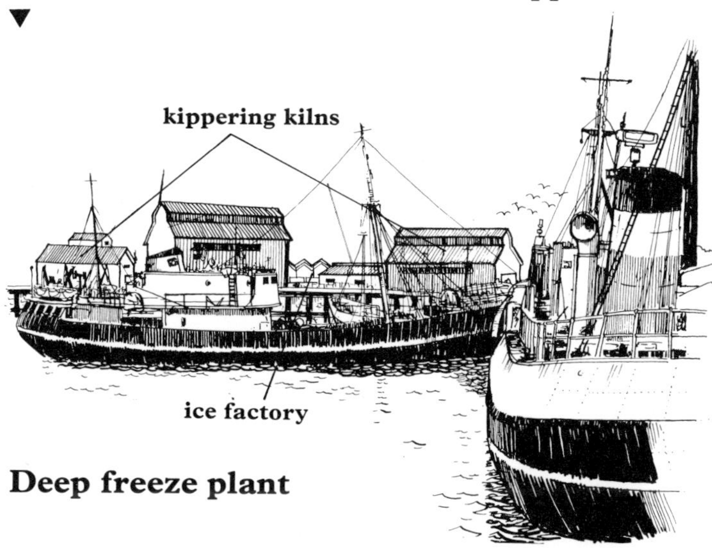

Deep freeze plant

Deep freeze plants are often found in fishing ports in order to preserve fish products for shipping to distant towns.

Ships' chandlers

This is a shop supplying the crews of fishing boats with the essential goods they need such as ropes, lubricants and fuel oil. ◀

Ice factories

Quayside factories manufacturing ice are used to supply fishing boats with the ice they need to preserve the fish on board ship before they return to port.

Ports of registration

The port of registration of a fishing boat is usually indicated by the **registration letters** appearing on the sides of the boat. You can see examples in these pictures. Thus WK is WicK, AH is ArbroatH and TT is TarberT. Usually the first and last letters of the parent fishing port are taken. But the port is often obvious such as OB for Oban. ▼

COASTAL DEFENCES: PAST AND PRESENT

▲ **Fort of the Saxon Shore**

The vulnerability of the coast to invasion was recognised in medieval times and many **castles** were built on prominent coastal sites. The sea acted like a moat and in addition a hard-pressed garrison could always be relieved from the sea.

In earlier centuries **beacons** were lit to warn of invasions. Henry VIII built special **artillery forts** (see page 71). ▼

to FIRE BEACON HILL

In Roman times there were coastal attacks on Britain by Saxon pirates. To prevent them the Romans built ◀ **forts** and **warning stations** along the coast. The forts were known as "Forts of the Saxon Shore".

▶

▲ **Dover Castle**

Pill boxes and **barbed wire** and **prohibited beaches** are sometimes still to be seen at the coast reminding us of the dangers of invasion during the Second World War. ▶

▲ **Martello tower**

In the Napoleonic wars at the turn of the eighteenth and nineteenth centuries **Martello towers** were erected at the coast in southern England.

▲

At Fylingdales in Yorkshire an **early warning system** against nuclear attack has been erected.

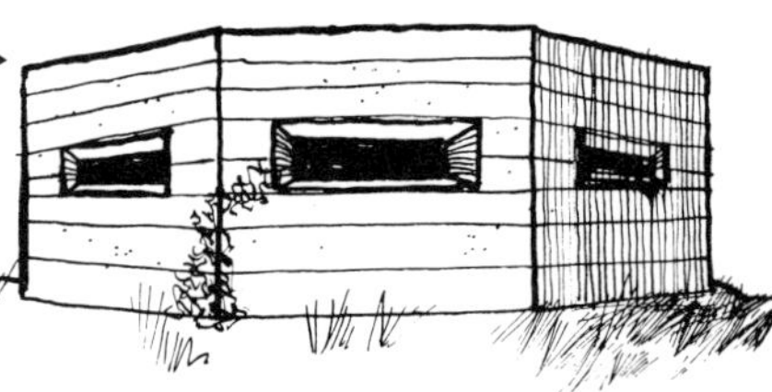

▲ **World War II pill box**

ALPHABETICAL INDEX

Major references are printed in capital letters.

PICTURE INDEX

POSTS

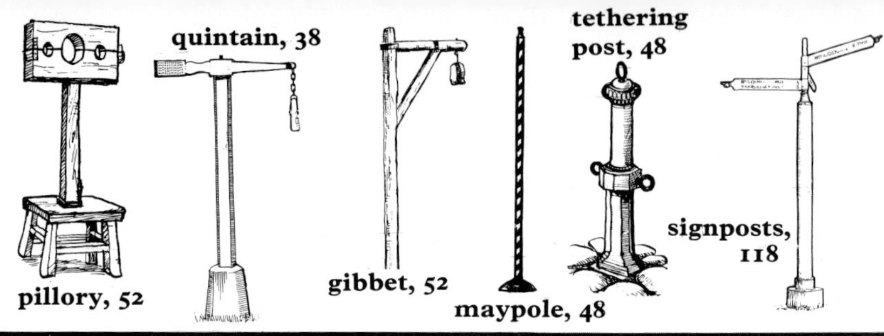

CROSSES OBELISKS AND STONE PILLARS

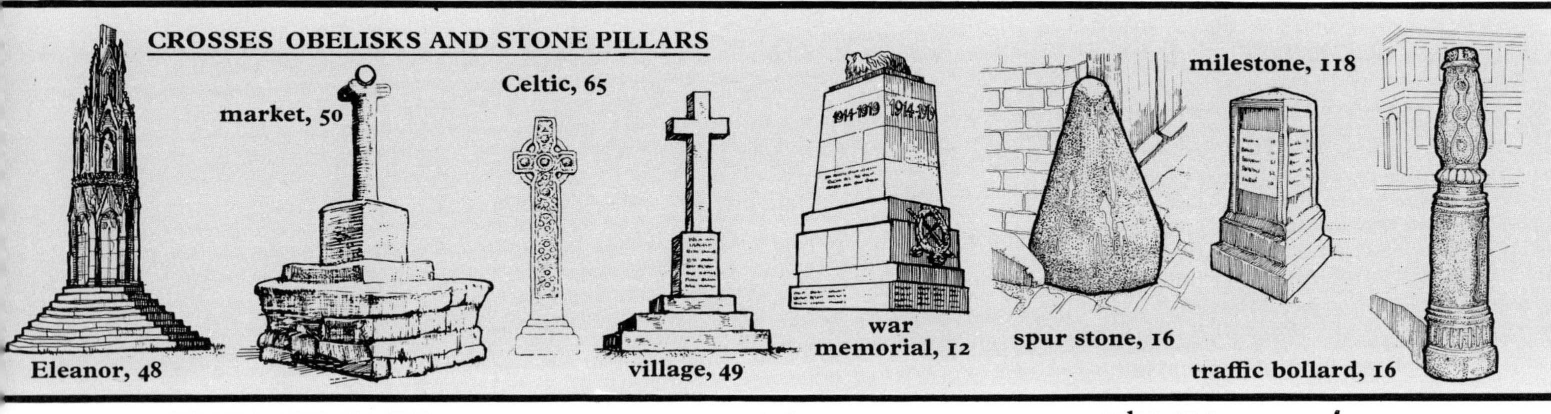

TOWERS AND MASTS

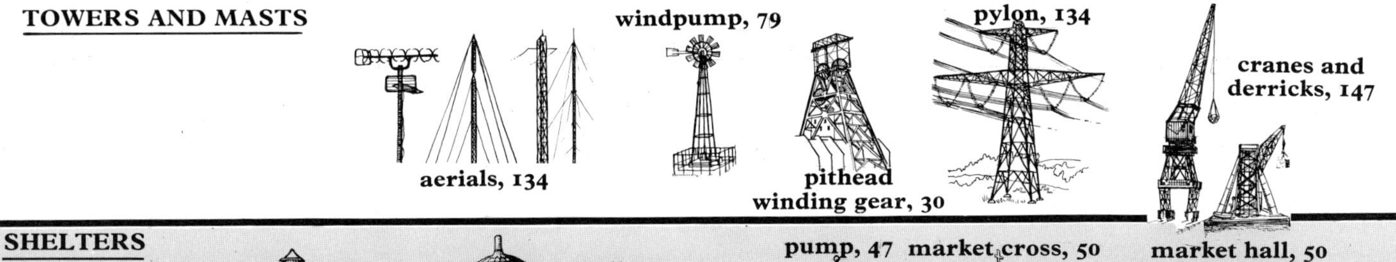

SHELTERS

WALLS

WALL FEATURES 56, 57, 83

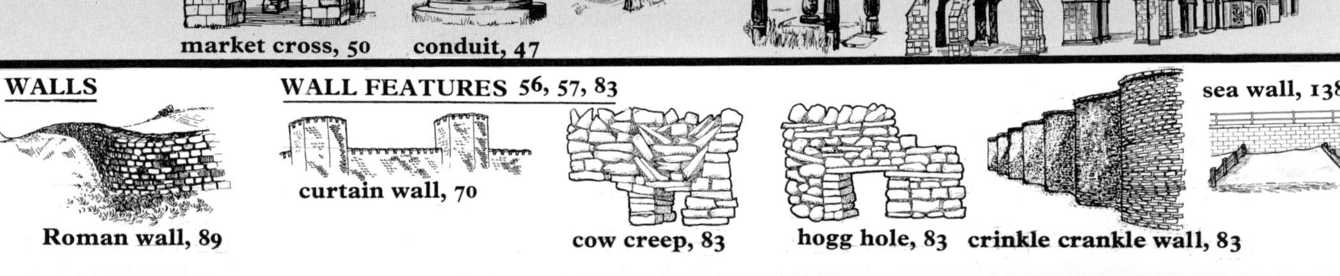

ROUND TOWERS

cooling towers, 31

broch, 85

martello tower, 154

oil storage tank, 32

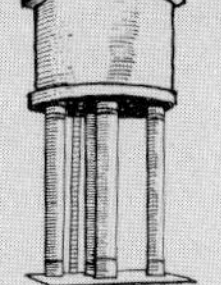
water tower, 47

oast house, 78

lime kiln, 35

smelt chimney, 35

silo, 78

pottery kiln, 35

blast furnace, 32

Irish round tower, 54

windmills, 36

lighthouses, 150-151

lock up, 53

dovecote, 48

rotunda, 19

baronial tower, 71

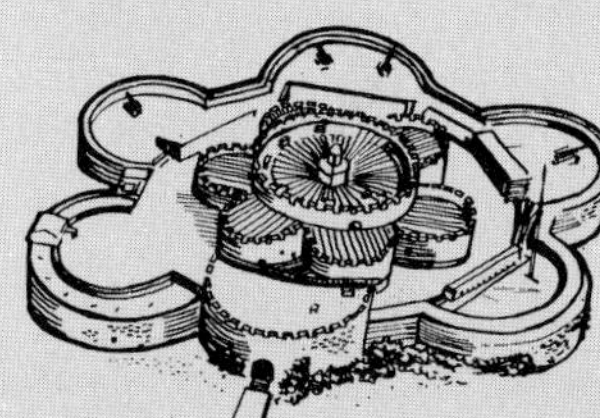
Tudor fort, 71

RECTANGULAR, SQUARE AND MANY-SIDED TOWERS

pele tower, 71

keep, 70

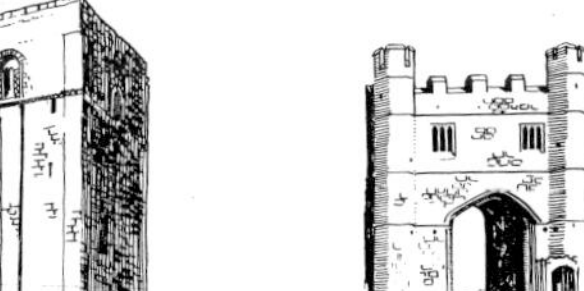
gatehouse, 13

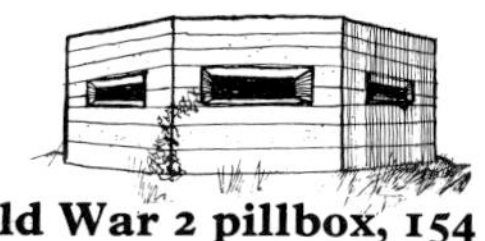
World War 2 pillbox, 154

lock up, 53

water tower, 47

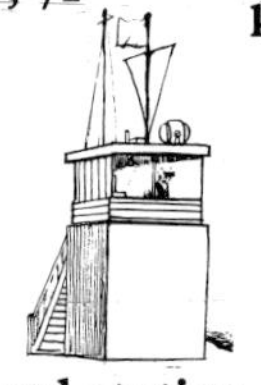
coastguard station, 151

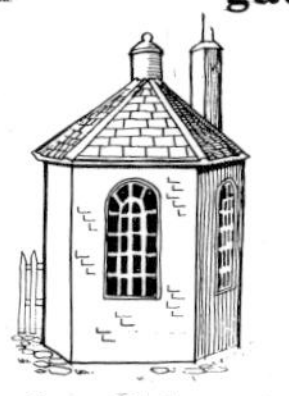
canal toll house, 128

road toll house, 123

tin mines, 35

lookout tower, 147

OTHER BUILDINGS

tithe barn, 78

barn on staddle stones, 78

water mill, 37

mews cottages, 17

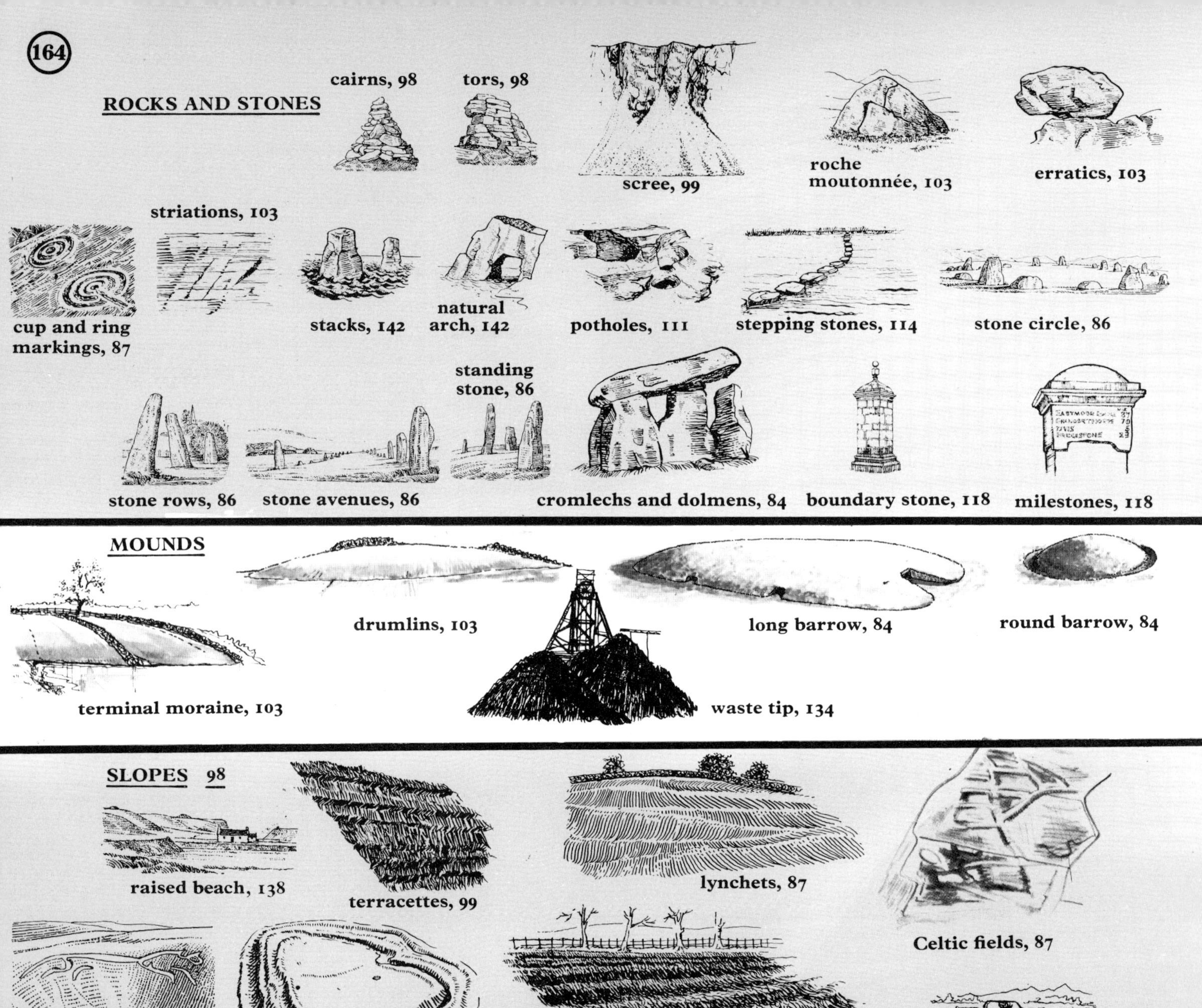
ROCKS AND STONES
cairns, 98
tors, 98
scree, 99
roche moutonnée, 103
erratics, 103
striations, 103
cup and ring markings, 87
stacks, 142
natural arch, 142
potholes, 111
stepping stones, 114
stone circle, 86
standing stone, 86
stone rows, 86
stone avenues, 86
cromlechs and dolmens, 84
boundary stone, 118
milestones, 118
MOUNDS
drumlins, 103
long barrow, 84
round barrow, 84
terminal moraine, 103
waste tip, 134
SLOPES 98
raised beach, 138
terracettes, 99
lynchets, 87
Celtic fields, 87
white horse, 87
hill fort, 85
ridge and furrow, 87
ha ha, 66

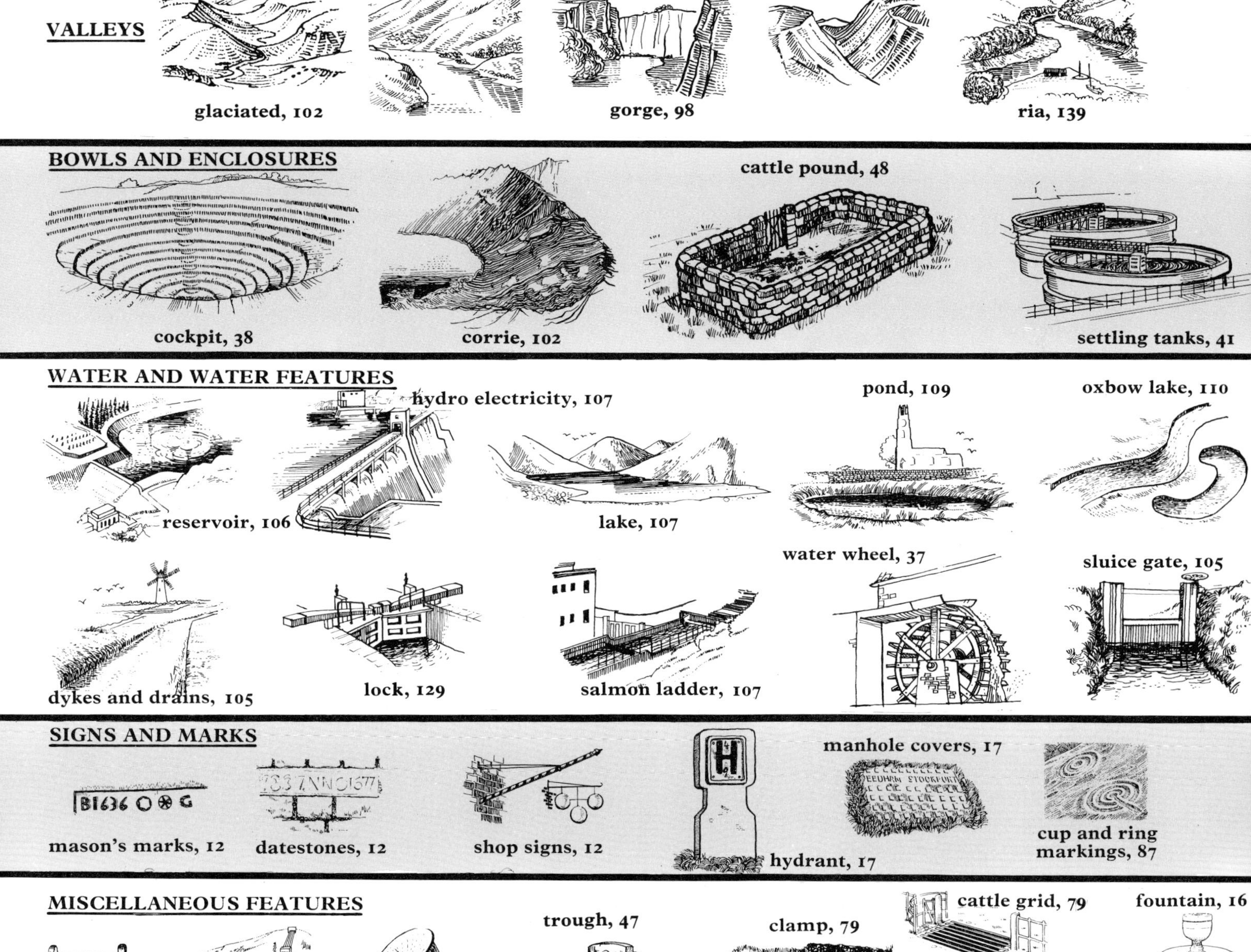
VALLEYS
glaciated, 102
fiord, 139
gorge, 98
river, 98
ria, 139
BOWLS AND ENCLOSURES
cockpit, 38
corrie, 102
cattle pound, 48
settling tanks, 41
WATER AND WATER FEATURES
reservoir, 106
hydro electricity, 107
lake, 107
pond, 109
oxbow lake, 110
dykes and drains, 105
lock, 129
salmon ladder, 107
water wheel, 37
sluice gate, 105
SIGNS AND MARKS
mason's marks, 12
datestones, 12
shop signs, 12
hydrant, 17
manhole covers, 17
cup and ring markings, 87
MISCELLANEOUS FEATURES
stocks, 52
hydro electric pipes, 107
radio telescope, 134
trough, 47
clamp, 79
cattle grid, 79
door scraper, 16
fountain, 16

Other books to read

The following books which were often consulted in the preparation of this book are invaluable sources of further reference if you want to find out more about particular topics which could be given only limited space here.

Pevsner, *The Buildings of England*—individual volumes covering all the English counties (Penguin)

Bray and Trump, *The Penguin Dictionary of Archaeology* (Penguin)

Fleming, Honour and Pevsner: *The Penguin Dictionary of Architecture* (Penguin)

How Things Work, Books 1 and 2 (Paladin)

Shire Publications *Discovering* Series (a vast range of titles from Abbeys to Zoos)

Vedel and Lange: *Trees and Bushes* (Methuen)

Methuen *Get to Know* Series (*Parish Church*; *Factories and Workshops*; *Farms*; *Houses and Flats*; *Inland Waterways*; *Post and Telegraph*; *British Railways*; *Water Supply*; *Roads and Streets*; *Boundaries*; *Bridges*; *Village Survey*; *Docks and Harbours*; *Country Town Survey*; *Shops and Markets*)

Collins *Field Guides* (*Insects*; *Trees*; *Sea Shore*; *Animal Tracks and Signs*; *Archaeology*; *Mammals*; *Butterflies*; *Birds*; *Wild Flowers*; *Mushrooms and Toadstools*)

Blandford Colour Series (*Fossils*; *Minerals and Rocks*; *Insects*; *Mountain Flowers*; *Nesting Birds*; *Woodland Life*; *Poisonous Plants and Fungi*; *Mushrooms and Toadstools*; *Pocket Encyclopaedia of Wild Flowers*)

Warne's *Observer's Books* (*British Birds*; *Architecture*; *Wild Flowers*; *Trees and Shrubs*; *Freshwater Fishes*; *Common Insects and Spiders*; *Grasses*; *Sedges and Rushes*; *Geology*; *Ferns*; *Butterflies*; *Wild Animals*; *Common Fungi*; *Flags*)

Hamlyn's Little Guides (*Ferns*; *Mosses and Fungi*; *Birds*; *Birdwatching*; *Rocks and Minerals*; *Sea Shells*; *Caves and Caving*; *Fossils*; *Mammals*; *Trees*; *Zoology*; *Fishes*; *Insects*; *Mushrooms*; *Wild Flowers*)

Visual History of Modern Britain (*Industry and Technology*; *Transport*; *The Town*; *House and Home*; *The Land*; *Government*) (Studio Vista)

On Location Series (*Churches*; *Castles*; *Museums*; *Roads*; *Railways*; *Rivers*; *Sea Coast*; *Canals etc.*) (Mills and Boon)

Automobile Association, Reader's Digest Association and Drive Publications (*Book of the British Countryside*; *Treasures of Britain*; *Folklore Myths and Legends*; *The Reader's Digest AA Book of the Road*; *AA Illustrated Guide to Britain*; *AA Book of the Seaside*; *The AA Illustrated Road Book of England and Wales*; *The AA Illustrated Road Book of Scotland*; *The Reader's Digest Atlas of the British Isles*)

Shell Books and Guides (*England*; *Scotland*; *Wales*; *Ireland*; *Britain*; *Exploring Britain*; *Country Alphabet*; *Bird Book*; *Country Book*)

Sauvain: *First Look at Maps* (Watts); *A Map Reading Companion*; *A Geographical Field Study Companion*; *Exploring at Home*; *Lively History* Series Books 1-4; *Practical Geography* Series, Books 1-4 (Hulton); *On a Farm*; *By Land, Sea and Air*; *Under Your Feet*; *On Holiday*; *Dial 999*; *In Town*; *Back in the Past*; *Made in Britain* (Macmillan)

Leutscher: *Ecology* Series (*Water Life*; *Towns*; *etc*); *The Seashore* (Watts).

Watts *First Look* Series (*Birds*; *Flowers*; *Heraldry*; *etc*)

Bull: *A Town Study Companion*; *A Rural Studies Companion* (Hulton)

Oxford Atlas of Britain and Northern Ireland (Oxford)

Dictionary of English Place Names (Oxford)

Polunin: *Concise Flowers of Europe* (Oxford)

Keble Martin: *Concise British Flora in Colour* (Ebury Press and Michael Joseph)

Harris & Lever: *Illustrated Glossary of Architecture* (Faber)

Bannister Fletcher: *History of Architecture* (Batsford)